THE
GROUP
HOUSE
Handbook

*"THE GROUP HOUSE HANDBOOK: How to Live
with Others (and Love It!)* . . . could prove a godsend.
This invaluable and innovative guide will tell you
everything you need to know, from how to find and
finance a group house to how to keep it running
smoothly.*"*
—New Age Magazine

THE GROUP HOUSE Handbook

by Nancy Brandwein, Jill MacNeice
and Peter Spiers

illustrated by Loel Barr

ACROPOLIS BOOKS LTD.
Washington, D.C.

640
B821
A-1

ACROPOLIS BOOKS LTD.
Colortone Building, 2400 17th St., N.W.
Washington, D.C. 20009

Printed in the United States of America by
COLORTONE PRESS, Creative Graphics Inc.
Washington, D.C. 20009

ATTENTION: Schools and Corporations
ACROPOLIS books are available at quantity discounts with bulk purchase for educational, business, or sales promotional use. For information, please write to: SPECIAL SALES DEPARTMENT, ACROPOLIS BOOKS LTD., 2400 17th ST., NW, WASHINGTON, D.C. 20009

Are there ACROPOLIS Books you want but cannot find in your local stores?
You can get any Acropolis book title in print. Simply send title and retail price, plus 50¢ per copy to cover mailing and handling costs for each book desired. District of Columbia residents add applicable sales tax. Enclose check or money order only, no cash please, to:
ACROPOLIS BOOKS LTD.,
2400 17th ST., NW
WASHINGTON, D.C. 20009

OR SEND FOR OUR COMPLETE CATALOGUE OF ACROPOLIS BOOKS.

Library of Congress Cataloging in Publication Data

Brandwein, Nancy, 1958-
    The group house handbook.

    Bibliography: p.
    Includes index.
    1. Communal living—United States. 2. Housing,
Cooperative—United States. I. MacNeice, Jill, 1956-
II. Spiers, Peter, 1955-   . III. Title.
HQ971.B72 1982 640 82-16475
ISBN 0-87491-090-0 (pbk.)

THE GROUP HOUSE BOOK

A C K N O W L E D G E M E N T S

O ur gratitude to the many, many people whose stories, advice and wisdom culled from years (days, even) of group living contributed to the making of this book.

Our special thanks and appreciation to Al Hackl, Kathleen Hughes and Laurie Tag for their encouragement, guidance and understanding and to the rest of the Acropolis staff who cheered us along: Allyson Everngam, John Hackl, Robert Hickey, Jody Peskin, Sandy Trupp and David Uslan.

Our appreciation for the time, support and valuable contributions of: David Anderson, Elizabeth Arnold, Susan Bennett, Carol Brandwein, Julianne Cline and her children, John Diamantes, Elizabeth Fox, Jenny and Sara Hughes, Steve Jordan, Beth Meer, Ana Montes, Betsy Neal, Don Thomas, Jim Welsh, and, of course, the crew at 3319 16th St., N.W.

Last, but certainly not least, our thanks to those close to us who "made it all possible": Helen and David Brandwein, the MacNeices, and Sarah Smedley Spiers.

CONTENTS

In the twelve years the three of us have spent collectively in group houses, we have seen friendships form, de-form, and re-form and felt all the joy and pain of alliances shifting within the group. We have watched love affairs flare up and fade, become brilliant marriages, or smolder on for years, unfulfilled. We have experienced extraordinary moments, times we will always remember: that snowy evening we stayed up all night drinking wine and playing a hilarious round of charades; the slow Sunday morning we lingered over a pot of coffee, a batch of fresh corn muffins, and *The New York Times*, staging a mock battle over who would get the crossword puzzle. We have also weathered those desperate days when our patience was pinched to the breaking point and things seemed like they would never again be right. Yet we lived to tell the tale.

We have come to realize that most people enter group living blindly, out of necessity or the vague idea that sharing a house with others would be fun. At least we did. Then suddenly we found ourselves thrown together with strangers; some of them were people we had never known, others were old friends that we began to know differently. With each person came all the accompanying quirks and qualities, passions and peeves—sometimes for better but many times for worse.

"If only I had known what I was getting into when I moved here," house members told us over and over. Those words echo our own thoughts. If only! A tall order, perhaps, but it is the germ of our book. With the proverbial 20/20 vision that comes from hindsight, we offer you here a book of advice.

There is another reason for writing this book. We wanted to chronicle a lifestyle we feel is greatly misunderstood. We wanted to bring it into the open, to make it public, and in the process, to combat popular prejudice. "Oh, you live in a *group* house!" people would say to us with an indulgent smile, as if group living were somehow synonymous with group sex. It is not, of course. This is not to say that such things never happen in group houses, but they certainly take place with no greater frequency than among people who have their own apartments. The point is, there is nothing horrible, frightening, odd, disgusting, or decadent about people who share a house. Some of our best friends do. No doubt, some of yours do too.

In case you are wondering, many of the situations we describe came directly from our own experience, unembellished. Much of our information also came from interviews. In our study of group living, we talked to hundreds of group house dwellers from around the country, people who spoke to us candidly but in all confidentiality about their situations and their feelings. To assure anonymity, we have given them new names and occupations, occasionally new residences.

Humor, as you will see, is an important part of our book, as it is in any shared arrangement. For a house without humor is a wooden world indeed. We learned this the hard way. Yet despite the stresses and strains, we have found group houses to be remarkably resiliant environments—if you want them to be. Of course, no handbook can magically make you get along better with others, but we've learned a trick or two and picked up some others. They are presented to you here, to help you over the rough spots and, we hope, tickle a few fancies in the process.

Nancy
Jill
Peter

September, 1982

Living With Others (And Loving It!)

You don't have to be a student or eat granola to live in a group house: lawyers and librarians, sculptors and seniors, teachers, toddlers, carpenters and computer programmers are sidestepping traditional family arrangements to set up housekeeeping with others.

By trading the frontier virtue of self-sufficiency for the interdependence of a cooperative lifestyle, these people share expenses and space and a bit of themselves. Together they form a group house—a living situation that is cheaper than an apartment, more congenial than a boarding house, less confining than a commune.

Group living makes sense for a number of

reasons. The cost of housing has increased 75 percent in the last five years. The average price of a single-family house in 1981 was about $75,000, according to the National Association of Realtors. The rental situation is not much better. A one-bedroom apartment in one of the nation's larger cities can cost $400 a month and can be even higher in a particularly desirable neighborhood. In fact, housing is so expensive that the rule of thumb that puts rent at one-third of a person's income is outmoded. Many people now pay as much as half their earnings for housing.

According to the Worldwatch Institute, a research organization based in Washington, D.C., this is only the beginning. "The cost of housing is going to soar," predicted Bruce Stokes, author of the institute's study on the global housing situation. "Shared housing arrangements are going to be necessary . . . and it's not just a question of lifestyle." He said that factors such as the cost of land, building materials, energy, and capital will continue to climb, "pushing us into new kinds of living arrangements, including low-rise multi-family dwellings and shared housing."

To cope with this trend, more and more people are pooling their resources and living in groups. They are moving into the country's stock of large, comfortable, expensive houses or apartments, older structures with high ceilings, ornate fireplaces, and the expansive charm of a time when energy was cheap and help plentiful. "Who else are you going to rent an eight-bedroom house to but a group?" said Susan Bennett, a Washington D.C. real estate agent, echoing the sentiments of many agents across the country.

It isn't just the economics of a skyrocketing housing market that brings people together. They seek group living for convenience and companionship as well. "I make enough money to live on my own, but I prefer a group," said Steven, 28, a landscape architect who has lived in shared houses for almost a decade. "It's much easier to share the cooking and cleaning and more enriching to live with others."

Although the average family consists of 2.8 persons in a suburban house, more and more Americans are choosing alternative living situations. Later marriages, smaller families, working women who postpone childbirth, and a climbing divorce rate contribute to the atomization of the nuclear family on one hand, and the search for new forms of intimacy and support on the other. The group house with its combination of interdependence and independence has become an increasingly popular response to this modern social development.

At the same time, morals have changed to the point that it is acceptable, even desirable, for unrelated people of the opposite sex to live together. When Ann, a Cincinnati journalist, told her family about the house she was sharing with six other people, her grandfather wanted to know how she managed to round up so many single women. "We have both men and women," she explained tentatively, unsure what his response would be. Her grandfather thought about it a minute, then replied; "Oh, you mean like the television show 'Three's Company?' " And it was clear he understood.

While the Census Bureau doesn't collect information about group houses per se, it does have figures on the so-called "nonfamily households," that is, unrelated people living together, be they couples or groups, lovers or strangers. According to the most recent count, a quarter of all households, more than 3 million Americans, are comprised of unrelated people.

In 1978 and largely in response to this phenomenon, Census Bureau demographer Arthur Norton coined the term POSSLQ— an acronym for "Partners of the Opposite Sex Sharing Living Quarters." POSSLQ does not necessarily refer to live-in lovers. Norton would also include a widow of advanced age who rents a room to a young college student. Census statistics show that the number of POSSLQs in the United States has tripled in the past decade. Yet POSSLQs are not the only ones who choose to live in group situations. Single parents, married couples, indeed, whole families have sought shared housing. By combining personalities and possessions, they create a whole that is far greater than the sum of its parts.

The benefits of such situations are virtually limitless. Equally limitless are the pitfalls. Sharing, compromise, communication—the same qualities essential to good family life—are also important in group houses. Unlike families, groups do not have a pre-arranged, universally accepted structure for authority and responsibility. There are no Mom and Pop to lay down the law, no children to test it. Put another way: while all families are group houses, all group houses are not families. So each shared house must evolve its own delicate system based on the inclinations of the members, individuals who may have very different ideas about the way things should be done. In many ways, the secret to successful group living is in learning how to thread your way through the maze of other peoples' idiosyncracies without compromising your own. Hopefully, the members will share what one veteran group house dweller called "an underlying agreement to agree."

Although no two set-ups are alike, group houses share certain regulating principles and mechanisms. *The Group House Handbook* is designed to uncover the systems that keep shared situations healthy. It lays out the alpha and the omega of group life. It deals with the nitty gritty: money, sex, the law.

If you're thinking of setting up or moving into a group house, if you live in one now that could stand some change, or if you're simply an armchair voyeur, *The Group House Handbook* will prove a valuable tool. It will provide you with a firm foundation of information culled from hundreds of interviews, extensive research, and firsthand experience. The chapter on starting a house from scratch and finding compatible housemates, has tips on how to interview. Another section deals with household organization and covers everything from group finances to house meetings.

The handbook goes into the inevitable conflicts that center on food and cleaning, as well as the added concerns over how to deal with visitors and pets. It includes illustrations from some more successful and some not so successful systems for your clarification and edification. Buying your group house is also touched on, as is dealing with the unique situation of the owner who is also a housemate. Insurance, zoning, and landlord-tenant relations are described in detail.

A special section focuses on group-housing for seniors—an increasingly popular alternative to the nursing home. The book contains a complete guide to senior and intergenerational arrangements, including a listing of resources.

Finally, throughout the book are essays on "advanced group living," that is, the parties, outings, and special projects that can make group living in your house an exciting, memorable experience.

What Is A Group House?

Some people call them urban communes, others call them shared or cooperative houses. However, the term "group house" seems most useful because it is broad enough to cover many different kinds of shared living arrangements, ranging from closely knit groups with common goals to random collections of people who go pretty much their own way.

Unlike the word "commune" with its counter-culture connotations, "group house" means nothing more than what it says: a group of individuals who live together. Not quite a community, not exactly an organization, and not really a family, a group household can be defined as:

- A space—a house, an apartment or loft
- shared by three or more people, including friends, strangers, couples, and children

- who all contribute time and money to maintain the living quarters, although not necessarily in equal amounts;
- and who share kitchen facilities, while not always sharing food.

The degree of sharing is something the members of each group house must work out for themselves. Sharing is a key concept in group houses, and it surfaces again and again—now as the basis for a strong spiritual bond among people, now as the source of seemingly insoluble problems. Just as traditional families must work out their own systems of sharing, so must each group house. In the absence of familial ties, though, the sharing takes on an even greater importance.

It is this emphasis on sharing, almost an ideology, that connects today's group houses and yesterday's communes with those American experiments in communal living that are every bit as old as the rugged individualism they shun.

The Link With The Past

Consider the cavemen: a handful of hoary humans huddling in the mouth of a cave created, in effect, the first group house. In those days, things were much simpler. No one argued about whose turn it was to take out the trash or what show to watch on television. No one worried about paying bills on time or buying an extra refrigerator. People just threw their lots together, chased saber-toothed tigers, rooted around for berries and wild asparagus, and that was that. Of course, there was not much need for a group house handbook. The infinite variety and subtlety of present day group living had not yet evolved.

Ever since man learned to say "I do," families have dominated the social scene. But by the 19th century, a number of shared living experiments had cropped up in this country that stretched the definition of family to include all group members, regardless of bloodline. The first and perhaps best known were the Shakers, a religious sect from England that migrated to the New World in the 1770s. Led by "Mother" Ann Lee, the matriarch who considered herself Christ's female counterpart, the Shakers established austere communities where believers held all material goods in common and lived together in large houses in groups of up to ninety people. Shakers, for the most part, practiced celibacy, so the men and women were segregated by floors.

Another experiment, the Oneida community, was founded in New York by John Noyes in the mid-19th century. Like the Shakers, Oneidans shared possessions and lived toegether in a large structure. Instead of celibacy, however, Oneidans adhered to a system called complex marriage, an arrangement by which all members were "married" to each other and older members of the community initiated the younger members into the mysteries of sex. The practice led to a sexual scandal and Oneida's eventual disintegration.

A number of utopias have blossomed and faded since the Oneida experiment. Then in the 1960s and 1970s the concept of retreat from the world with shared possessions and living quarters enjoyed a revival as Americans donned dungarees and headbands to live the simple life on communes in the countryside. Although the number of communes and the number of people living on them have dwindled since that time, a few still survive. There is, for example, "The Farm" in Tennessee, a vast vegetarian commune where hundreds of people live and work together tending crops, building and repairing structures, and taking care of all the members of their extended family.

Of course, group houses of the 1980s are somewhat different from the early utopian communities and the communes, but the mechanisms and problems are still the same. After all, somebody has to do the dishes, whether they be Shakers, hippies, or young professionals. Furthermore, all these living arrangments are built on the common belief that people can lead fuller, more pleasant, and at the very least, more affordable lives if they share their resources.

The reasons people live in group settings today are as varied as the people themselves. Some, who are drawn together for ideological purposes, make houses of environmentalists, Christians, political activists, or artists. Others seek friendship and stability in a cold, indifferent world. Still others set up housekeeping for mutual aid, because they think they will grow from the experience or for economic considerations. Group living motivated strictly by economic considerations, however, can turn out rather like an arranged marriage. Often, people come together for a combination of reasons.

While the group house down the street may not be a direct descendant of the American utopian experiments, it is at least a distant cousin.

Living with Others—and Loving It

"A lot of people walk around with the assumption that living alone is nirvana, that when you have enough money, you get your own place," said Susan, 25, who has lived in group houses for over five years. "But I think of my widowed mother who lives by herself and is terribly lonely. It's much nicer to have people to come home to."

In Washington D.C., one of the most expensive cities in the country, Susan pays living expenses of only $250 a month. The price includes rent, utilities, telephone and food—as well as the fireplaces, crystal chandeliers, and Oriental carpets of her Embassy Row house. She also gets the companionship of her eight housemates, people to chat about her day with, catch an occasional movie with, make her a pot of tea when she's sick, and loan her money in a pinch. "It would be horrible to live alone," she said.

The economics of group living speaks for itself. With a little patience, a little luck, and a bit of compromise, it is possible to live in a group house for as little as $170 a month, which includes about $100 for rent, $20 for utilities, $40 for food, and $10 for the telephone and extras. Of course, you may not be living in the most beautiful house, or in the best neighborhood, or in the most exciting city, but it can be done.

Debra, Doug, and Jeff, former students at Brown University, bought an abandoned house together in East Providence, Rhode Island, for $1,000. They took out a loan for another $15,000 to renovate the place, a 24 bedroom house that needed extensive repair. In addition to paying $150 a month for rent and food, each person who lives in the house contributes a day of work each week. It's a subsistence economy, and one winter the house was without heat altogether, but such an arrangement of group sweat equity is one inexpensive way to live.

On the other hand, some group houses are so well endowed that the members, quite well off in their own right, live like kings together. Four well-paid economists at the World Bank in Washington kick in $750 a month to rent their $2,000 a month Georgetown house. The extra money goes for frills—the cook, the maid, the well-stocked wine cellar, the lavish dinner parties.

However, even those on modest incomes can live quite comfortably as a group. Brian, a bearded environmental activist in Madison, Wisconsin, who makes only $8,000 a year, and his four like-minded housemates can still afford the comforts of a washing machine, a clothes dryer, a woodworking shop, a darkroom, and a car. "All these benefits you gain by cooperative living and sharing," he said. "Economically I couldn't make it alone in this city."

Other reasons people cite for group living range from security considerations, to better nutrition, to personal growth:

Women especially like group houses because they feel safer. I feel much better having men around.

I'd never cook if I lived alone.

I think it's healthy to live with other people. I learned to stick up for myself, yet at the same time be flexible about dealing with others. I learned how to cope with all kinds of people, and became stronger for it.

Tad, who is studying English at the University of Virginia at Charlottesville, likes his group house—called "The Ranch"—because it offers a community spirit to counterbalance those long hours in the library. The dorms, he said, are too impersonal. "If you're depressed, there's always someone to do things with. We have a certain identity, a sense of fellowship, a feeling of community."

Along with the easy camaraderie of group living can come an added boon: the sharing of skills. For example, Phil, 30, a video producer in New York, acted as house resume consultant. In return, his housemate Alan taught him how to fix cars. On the weekends, Phil would team up with another housemate, also involved in video, to film shows. Once they dressed up in costume and shot a Chekhov play.

Then there are those unexpected benefits. "My roommate John was really attractive and could pick up women anywhere," said Brad, as he began his oft-told tale about group houses. "One night, John picked up two women at a bar, and one of them jumped into bed with me when I was asleep. I tell you, there are some real advantages to group living!"

Of course, most of the sharing in group houses takes place on a much more commonplace level. Men who have never cooked before learn confidence in the kitchen. Women get lessons in bicycle repair. Paul, who was applying to law school last year, got a preview of his future life when he moved into a house full of law students. "It was great," he recalled. "I could grill them on anything."

Although people in Paul's house are fairly independent, bumping into each other over the breakfast table or during dinner, other groups make more of an effort to spend time together. They strive to create an atmosphere of warmth and mutual caring that is very much like a family.

Katie and Al, who have been married for seven years, have such a situation with three other close friends in Philadelphia. "We have created a family structure for ourselves, a source of support, and we're not just in this for economic reasons," said Katie. "What is important is that we share and support each other and are committed to relating to each other in a very intimate way."

This support and intimacy brought Katie smoothly through a recent operation and carried another housemate through her first performance as a professional dancer. On the mantlepiece in Katie's spacious house are snapshots of the group on outings, at the beach, picking apples in the fall, at a costume party, during their annual Thanksgiving dinner ritual.

Dominique's house is another example of a group as an expanded family arrangement. When she came to the United States from France two years ago, the transition to a totally new culture was eased by living with others. Her American housemates helped Dominique learn English more quickly; and now, although she could afford to live alone, she prefers her group situation. She prefers it because of the warm family atmosphere it offers.

"I have, in a sense, constructed the family I always wanted," she confessed. Raised as an only child, Dominique longed for a big family. Now, with four other housemates, all older, all men, she has it. "We tease each other constantly," she said. "I think of the guys as older brothers."

Divorce is another reason people turn to group living. A group house can be the perfect counterbalance to the isolation of married life and the trauma of ending it.

"The first months were very difficult for me," recalled Harry, a bearded history professor who moved to Chicago when he separated from his wife three years ago. "I was alone in a new city. A friend suggested I try a group house for a while, until I got my feet on the ground. At first I thought he was kidding. But I answered an ad and liked the people, so I moved in. I was only there a year, but it was an excellent transition for me. And I made some good friends in the process."

Ellen, 32, a recently divorced nursing student, moved into a group house for the support it offered. "I was very dependent on my husband," she said. "When we got divorced, all our friends turned out to be his friends. I just didn't have that much of a support system. So I decided to move into a group house, and it's really helped me over the rough spots. I find that people live in group houses because they are into getting support and being supportive."

Helen, also recently divorced, found herself with a six-bedroom house and not enough money to pay the mortgage. Although it was more space than she needed because her three children were old enough to be living on their own, Helen was determined to keep the house. First one friend moved in and then another and soon her house was full of rent-paying people.

"I really loved the place, had lived there for two decades," Helen said. "Besides, I needed the company. My whole family was scattered. For awhile that house was the only thing I had. I just couldn't give it up."

Group living is not just for singles. Many couples have found that sharing a house adds a much-needed social balance to the intensity of marriage.

"Married people tend to become too wrapped up in each other," said Mark, a Washington-based computer consultant who lives with two other couples in a house in suburban Northern Virginia. "I love my wife, but I want close relationships with others as well. But if I didn't live with my friends, I'd probably never see them." His wife Connie likes the arrangement too because she has companionship when Mark, who travels frequently, is away from home.

Even people with young children are finding that group houses offer an attractive environment for parenting. Mothers with infants and toddlers, for example, get companionship and some one who will share babysitting and shopping duties. Older children get extra input and attention from being around the other adults in group houses.

"I would definitely recommend a group house for children," said Kimberly, 37, a divorced woman who lives in a group house with her eight-year-old son and five-year-old daughter. "I just don't think parents can give their children a complete picture of the world. I enjoy seeing my housemates talking to the kids about their different interests, even when they present a viewpoint I don't necessarily have. I'm glad that my children are exposed to it."

Kimberly also thinks that group living gives children a healthy respect for others that they might not learn until much later in life. "It's important for the children to get feedback from other adults," she said. "A lot of times, their mother is tuned out. But if someone else tells them to be quiet, they really listen."

Not only the young but also the very old and the handicapped benefit from shared living. Group houses for senior citizens are much less expensive and far more pleasant than nursing homes. Sharing a house can be a welcome alternative for those who are healthy enough to take care of themselves but are perhaps too old to be living totally alone. Maggie Kuhn, founder of the Gray Panthers and activist for the elderly, has turned her Victorian Philadelphia house into an intergenerational group residence.

"I love the vitality of these young people," she has written in *50 Plus* magazine about her group house. "Having them around re-energizes me, makes me feel more alive. What I have to offer them, hopefully, is a sense of experience and survivorship which can help give perspective to their lives. . . . Based on my twenty years of experience, I am certain that real friendship can exist between the generations."[1]

All over the country, organizations are springing up that set up and sponsor senior group houses because these new arrangements help to alleviate the isolation seniors feel in our society. One man in his late sixties, Larry, a retired army officer, while wary of changing his well-established routine, felt nostalgic for the friendships he had enjoyed in his middle age. He sought help from a Boston community service group and moved in with two other retirees whom he enjoys "arguing with and taking meals together." For the old, then, as well as the young, group living provides a compromise based on the ideal of interdependence.

"House/Apartment To Share": Finding A House & Housemates

When rebellious youths of twenty years ago threatened to run off and join a commune, they had no doubts that the commune would accept them. Well, now you can't drop yourself at the doorstep of a group house and assume that they'll take you in. Often you will have to go through a rather structured process of screening before you are even considered as a housemate. Furthermore, people don't "run off" to live in group houses—at least not without first scanning the "House/Apt. To Share" column of the classifieds, now an institution in major dailies around the country.

Taking a Long Hard Look Before You Leap

Of course people feel an urgency when they're looking for a new living situation. In fact, there's a tendency among both house and housemate hunters to rush through this part of group living. You may feel pressured to rush into group life:

- You're unhappy in your present situation.
- You can't afford to live alone anymore.
- Your job requires you to move to a new city where you don't know a soul.
- Your college requires you to move out of the dorms after freshman year.

You think, What does it matter *how* I go about finding housemates. I just need a place to live. I'll work out the details later.

You will be better off working out the details now because a group house is much more than a "place to live." It's a place where, at the risk of losing some independence, you can lead a richer existence, both materially and emotionally. In a group house, some of your qualities, which would be all but ignored by the walls of your studio apartment, will be brought out and quickened as you interact with others. In addition to circumstantial pressures, this very *potential* can cause some paralyzing urgency. What you might feel when looking for a suitable group house is akin to what a writer feels when staring at a blank page deciding which word to use. Making choices, whether for words or people, is difficult because it involves defining what you want, saying clearly things like:

> *I want to live with other people, but I want to maintain a life apart from theirs.*
> *I want to move into a supportive household of other women.*
> *I want to share food but I don't want to have to cook for others.*

Defining what you want before you enter a group house or start one will ultimately free you from having to spend days, weeks, and even years catering to the lifestyles and whims of other people. When you define what you want, you have the best chance of finding housemates you can live with in a physical setting you like.

Although every group house has its own personality, to narrow down the field you have to generalize enough to decide what type of household to enter or form. Here are some of the more prevalent kinds of group arrangements.

- A household in which all members are required to share certain values or beliefs, whether political or religious in nature.
- A household that has a family atmosphere suitable for nurturing children.
- A household that provides a support network for women, men, gays, lesbians, blacks, and so forth.
- A household composed of diverse yet companionable people who share food and household responsibilities although they don't share a common credo.
- A household formed more for the sake of convenience in which members share no more than rent and utilities.

Unless you have very specific desires and can readily see yourself living in one of these household types or in one of the many that fall in between, you should talk to as many group dwellers as possible. The interview process will give you a chance to scope out the spectrum of group possibilities, but your time is better spent in limiting that spectrum first.

It's time-consuming to sit down and go over your expectations, especially when you feel rushed by landlords, realtors, or the need to move out of your present quarters. But remember, it isn't necessary to define everything to the nth degree; you can't anticipate every situation in a group house. In the course of cooperative living, systems are born, die, revised, and reborn. The key word when entering a group house is *flexibility.* Be forever ready to change or compromise your well-thought-out expectations!

Starting a House from Scratch

If you want to keep the amount of compromising to a minimum, you should think of starting a house from scratch. Although definitely a more painstaking process than moving into an existing household, forming a group house can be much more worthwhile. If you are tired of living in places where you are forced to adapt your expectations to suit others, if you want to fill a house with your *own* things, or if you want to share quarters with another family, starting a house from scratch will enable you to set the tone.

Idealists are great ones for starting houses from scratch. The group house you live in now may have been started in the 1960s and 1970s by a group of people who were eager to experiment and put their communal ideas into practice. Idealism is not dead, even if it's the simple ideal of having a group of caring people living together and enjoying each other's company.

Whatever your reasons for forming a group house, you'll need to decide what comes first: the housemates or the house? Unless you can afford to put down about $1,000 or more for a month's rent and security deposit on a house or apartment, you will first have to find housemates to split the expenses.

The quickest and least complicated way of starting a house is to assemble from two to four people, a core group, who want to live together. Decide what type of household you want to have along with the various responsibilities involved in maintaining your house, go househunting, put down the money, *then* recruit more housemates to fill the extra rooms.

Core groups that start houses in this fashion are usually composed of friends or close acquaintances. Be wary about starting a house with your friends, though. Friends often feel they don't have to discuss the workings of the house, that it will all flow as smoothly as an afternoon outing. Admittedly, if your house is composed of friends instead of a random assortment of people, the atmosphere of intimacy will carry your house over many a rough spot—but only so far. Like an elastic band, intimacy between people seems to have an infinite ability to stretch beyond the late rent payments, the dirty kitchen, the stereo blasting at 1:00 a.m. Then, WHAM, it snaps, often wreaking more havoc and heartbreak among friends than mere acquaintances.

However friendly you are with housemates or however cosmically connected, there will always be external pressures and differences to face—demands on your time and money. It's better to lose a bit of spontaneity by haggling over the details first. One way to test your compatibility is to schedule a dry run. Time and space permitting, spend a whole week or even a weekend together as a "test run" so you can observe house dynamics in action. Do two people constantly grate on each other's nerves? Is there a frivolous spender coupled with people who count their coins?

Another popular way of starting a group house from scratch is to assemble a large number of people for the express purpose of forming a household. You can gather friends, acquaintances, virtual strangers, and fellow workers by spreading the word, putting ads in the newspaper or posting notices on community bulletin boards. Allyson, a shy dancer from Florida, told of how she gained five new acquaintances, a sunny bedroom, and a glassed-in porch when she moved to Washington, D.C.:

> *Jim, he actually had put down the money for the house's rent so he got about fifteen of us together in the house's living room. At that time, there was no furniture at all in it. Jim led the meeting, described the kind of house he wanted: one that wasn't very*

*cohesive, where everybody buys their own food, equal
number of men and women. It worked out very nicely
because people who were interested in forming that
kind of household where everyone takes turns cooking
found each other and left to form their own house.
The rest of us, all strangers who found out about the
house from a notice at the "Food for Thought"
bulletin board, agreed right then and there that we'd
live together.*

It's lucky in this instance that another group selected itself out because meetings of this kind can make those who don't fit in feel excluded. A way to circumvent this sticky problem is to call the meeting together to form more than one household. That way everyone's needs may be met, and you won't feel pressed to take on people as housemates just because they are there and you feel bad about excluding them. Proceedings for this type of gathering should be well organized. You'll have to spell things out much more clearly than if you had a small core group, and it would be to your advantage to have several meetings before you go househunting, not to mention a weekend "test run."

Lastly, you can rely on a third party, the roommate referral service, to help you find people interested in starting a group house. More about referral services later, but their main benefit is in handling the cumbersome task of screening.

Betsy Neal of Roommates Preferred, a model roommate referral service in Washington, D.C., says that she often finds herself matching people up who don't yet have a house. "We suggest they meet on neutral ground, though, that they go to a restaurant instead of one another's present place so they can get to know each other without intimidation. Chances are high they'll have something in common to talk about."

What you pay for when you use a roommate referral service in this instance is the increased chance of gathering people together who have more in common than they would have if they had come by way of an ad in the paper or word of mouth. Also, it's likely that people who use referral services care more about their living situation, enough to go through the added effort and expense.

Putting the "House" into "Group House"

Once you have enough people to qualify as a group, it's time to find your house. The first thing you'll have to decide is whether you want to be owners or renters.

Buying cooperatively is becoming more and more common. Families who can't afford their own home as well as financially solvent singles are doubling-, tripling-, and quadrupling-up with others to buy otherwise unaffordable homes. You might consider buying if you:

- Have young children and want a sense of permanence. After all, buying will be cheaper in the long run.
- Desire more freedom to make changes and repairs. Perhaps you've always had a yen to fix up a battered old house with close friends and relations.
- Are tired of making your landlord rich and are considering cooperative buying as an investment.

Whatever your reasons, buying a home with others is not something to leap into. If it's a definite option for you, skip to Chapter 6 for advice and tips.

For the majority of group house dwellers who tend to be migratory creatures without a lot of cash, renting is the most feasible choice. It is also a good idea to rent together first before you buy together. Finding a house or apartment to rent isn't such hard work when you've got a group of people to split it with. One group that needed to find housing in a short time assigned each member two realtors to visit, and they scoured the "House/Apt. to Rent" section of the classifieds. Before you scatter to shop and compare, it is wise to come up with some group "requirements" for your future abode. Consider:

- How much money is everyone willing to spend for rent?

- Where do you all want to live? Will you be close enough to each person's place of work or study? If you have cars, is there adequate parking? If you don't have cars, is there easy access to public transportation and to the grocery store?

- If you have children, think about what the local schools are like and whether there are other children in the neighborhood. Furthermore, what kind of neighborhood do you want or *not want* to live in?

- How much will you be spending to heat and cool your house? Also, canvass your future housemates about air conditioning. If you live in a place that gets very steamy during the summer months, the rising temperature could create rising tempers. Decide whether your group will be pro air conditioning or pro ventilation, and then look for a house that suits your preference.

- What kind of lease is everyone willing to sign: month to month, six months, a year, longer? For more about leases see Chapter 6.

The issue of heating and cooling costs is oft-neglected but extremely important. Celia told us how her housemates fell in love with a sprawling Victorian mansion. The rent was cheaper than cheap, since it was situated fifteen miles outside the city. Everybody was reaching for their checkbooks until Celia brought up the issue of utility costs. She had noticed that the house was poorly insulated and that fact, along with its high ceilings, would make for extremely high heating costs. They called the realtor to get an estimate of an average January heating bill. They found that with oil heating, their dream home was anything but a bargain.

One last point on finding your dream group house: if you all go to view a house that you've picked as a "finalist," try to look, as your mother might say, presentable. It's not just the realtor or landlord presenting the house to you but you presenting yourselves to them.

Using Your Resources

Forming a household and finding a house to suit your ideals is hard work. Some of you may prefer the less arduous method of entering group house life: you may want to find a house already "furnished" with housemates. But how do people who want rooms in existing households meet those with vacancies in their group house? There are a number of ways for group dwellers and prospective housemates to advertise and find out about openings: word-of-mouth, newspaper ads, bulletin boards, off-campus housing offices, and roommate referral services. To make things clearer, those who need housing are called *seekers* and those who have housing but need housemates are *sharers*.

Spreading the Word

Whether sharer or seeker, you should immediately spread the word about your situation as you would if looking for a job. Put up signs where you work, and talk about your housemate or housing needs at parties—preferably while you are sober, or you won't know who will show up at your doorstep the next day. If you belong to a club, put yourself on the agenda at the next meeting. One thing to be cautious about while you spread the word is telling your friends and friends-of-friends because you won't want to feel obligated to live with them. It can be much worse rejecting your friend than a total stranger, but if you maintain that your friendship might be saved by staying in separate quarters, then no one should get seriously offended. If, after much thought, you do want your friend to move in, don't forgo the interview process. The decision to accept someone into your house rests ultimately with you *and* your housemates. An interview can help prevent casualness from turning into a casualty for your group house.

Deciphering the Classifieds —Is it worth it for you?

> Group House 2 m/f to
> shr beaut 5 BR, 3 BA
> hse, own rm w/pvt
> bath, w/d, a/c fpl,
> $190 1/5 utils.
> 289-5900 eves.

If yu cn rd ths ad, yu cn fnd a gd grp hse. Well, it ain't necessarily so. On the sharer's side, running classified ads in a local or major daily is the least popular and least reliable method of finding housemates. The only thing a newspaper ad in a daily paper will give you is sheer volume. If you put an ad in the paper, then you must prepare yourself for an onslaught of callers. The phone will literally ring off the hook for the duration of your ad, especially when your house is in a desirable location. Beware! Sometimes people follow up group house ads just for sport. Occasionally someone will call a group house specifically to find out where you live and when you'll be home or, translated, when you won't be home and it's most convenient to rob you.

For seekers, however, the paper has one advantage. In the comfort of your temporary lodgings you'll be able to scan the "Houses and Apartments to Share" section, jot down numbers, make calls, and set up interviews in a matter of minutes. It all seems so simple until you show up for the interview and find you're the twenty-third person who has looked at the house with ten more people to go and it's only Saturday. The competition can be fierce. When you make your initial calls, those on the other end of the line often won't sound as delighted to hear from you as you expected. One person who spent a whole month interviewing but finally broke down and used a roommate referral service theorizes that running newspaper ads, especially in major cities, puts sharers on the defensive. They might not act like themselves when accosted by so many people all bouncing with enthusiasm to occupy the room:

> I absolutely *love* the bedroom.

> It's tiny, but I've always had a knack for sleeping in a fetal position.

It goes against the whole purpose of running the ad and scheduling interviews when sharers feel so exhausted and put upon that they can't be objective and open.

Another disadvantage for both sharers and seekers is the impersonality of newspaper ads. Once you decipher the cryptic messages in those tiny boxes, you've found out only the bare essentials. The ad performs the minimum amount of screening. Seekers who respond to it do so because of the price and location, not because of any possible compatibility. They will find out whether a house has a fpl (fireplace) or a/c (air conditioning), but not whether the inhabitants are E.G.F.P.W.L.C.M. (easy going friendly people who like classical music).

If you do go ahead and put an ad in the paper to make certain you cover the bases, then develop a thorough method of telephone screening. If you're up for it, one proponent of amassing housemates from the classifieds advises, "Interview as many people as you can stand, and then ask three or four of the prospects to come by again. That way, you aren't pressed to find *the ideal housemate* out of, say, thirty people."

The Alternative Press

In every city or college town there are scads of small local papers that can serve as more helpful sources for housemate selection than the major city papers can. The small papers have some advantages: narrower circulation, cheaper rates (so sharers can add more vital information about their house and household), and perhaps, a very specialized audience (e.g. gays, blacks, religious groups, holistic health advocates, feminists, leftists, and so on). However, if you can count on ads in the major papers to bring a "madding crowd" of the mainstream into your home, you can depend on the special interest press to bring you a smaller but "madder" crowd, people whose lives center around the very beliefs or values that a particular paper espouses. They may be overly concerned with world politics while neglecting the dire issues right under their noses, like the trash that hasn't been taken out in two weeks.

Taking Note of Notices

> Large friendly group house in Mt. Pleasant area needs male or female housemate to fill room in lovely Victorian mansion. We prefer vegetarian, non-smoking cat lovers, someone who wants to share food and cooking responsibility 4 nights a week. We are a diverse household with 1 masseuse, 1 artist, a market analyst who sky dives on weekends, and a currently unemployed government worker who is thinking of starting her own restaurant. The room is spacious and on the sunny side of the house. Rent is only $215 per mo plus util (but we don't believe in air conditioning). Open May 1. Call Larry or Roberta 682-5491.

This notice is typical of ones you'll find in local bookstores, restaurants, health food stores, bars, supermarkets, libraries, churches and on community bulletin boards. It's typed on an index card and features a crude but spirited drawing of said Victorian house, and it didn't cost a cent for the group house to put it up. The seekers who called Larry in response to the notice were indeed cat-loving, non-smoking vegetarians who cook. The sharers had five people from which to choose, but that was more than enough. The man who moved in had always wanted to learn how to sky dive.

On an index card, you have space enough to describe every notable nuance of your group house if you so choose. For seekers, such notices reveal much more about the inhabitants of group houses than do newspaper ads. Even the handwriting and format of the notice can come into play. For instance, you can always tell an organized household by its notice done up in resume form. Then there are the born salespeople who make tabs bearing their phone number at the bottom of the notice or the creative types who draw pictures of their house.

Another benefit of going the bulletin board route is that sharers can choose their "audience" simply by choosing where they post their notice. Do you want vegetarians? Then advertise for a housemate at the local health food store. Do you want parents? Then post your notice at a community or day-care center. Bulletin boards are not just standards at small counter-culture hangouts, as some people like to think; you find them in personnel offices, libraries, churches, and cafeterias too. Do some detective work to scope out where the kind of people you're looking for might be. Incidentally, sharers should involve the whole house in deciding what to say on the notice. Occasionally, one member of a house will write up prerequisites for the prospective housemate and then sneak off to post them. While all of you are figuring out what to put on the notice, it's a good time to redefine the various beliefs and responsibilities that go into making your house distinctive. Remember, however, to step down from your more philosophical requirements and include pedestrian items like the date of availability and your phone number.

Some people get even more then they bargain for when they post and respond to notices—a new friend, a business contact, a date for the evening. One woman, an accomplished graphic artist, spent several hours making her sign into a slick art-deco design. She xeroxed it on fuschia paper and tacked it up at all sorts of chic little boutiques in New York's Soho. She not only found a loft-mate, but she landed a job as a freelance designer. The man who put up notices for his house's vacancy on telephone poles in his suburban neighborhood was not so lucky. Saturday came, and he had a whole flock of neighbors waiting for his yard sale to begin.

Off-Campus Housing Offices

Mary, an Economics major from the University of Virginia, talks about her experience:

At the University of Virginia, they moved us out of the dorms after our first year. The other girls in my hall were teaming up, and though I could've gone in with three of them, I kept stalling, since—I guess—I didn't want to live with them that much. Also, they wanted to put our names in the lottery for the second year dorms, a monstrosity of high rise apartments set in a parking lot. Finally, I stole off to the off-grounds housing office and pored through the blue three-ringed notebook which had listings of people who had housing to share in it. Within about four days, I found three girls, virtual strangers, in an old house not far from my classes. It was neat starting fresh with people I didn't know after feeling like such an outsider on my hall.

For Mary and many other students, living off campus is a ticket to freedom. Yet students often feel unsure about how to enter this period between dormitory life and "the real world." That's why there are fraternities and sororities and off-campus housing offices. For those of you who don't want to go Greek, you'd be wise to step into your school's housing office. Anyway, the money it takes to run the office comes out of your tuition!

These offices are, in effect, resource rooms for sharers and seekers (not to be confused with roommate referral services). Offices at smaller colleges like the University of Virginia may have listings for both sharers and seekers housed in notebooks of contrasting colors. The University of Maryland, on the other hand, with its enrollment of 40,000 students offers computer printouts of available houses, apartments, and rooms categorized by their distance from the campus. All off-campus housing facilities are guaranteed to have helpful literature on the various types of housing you'll find in your area. Georgetown University, for instance, hands out a thick booklet on the local housing situation with a section on tips for the uninitiated.

Whether sharer or seeker, try to write between the lines on the housing office forms, which are by necessity rather terse. When filling out the form, scribble in comments or add a page of pertinent information about yourself or your house. Be sure to note the study/party habits you prefer in a housemate. The study/party issue is a common denominator in most student houses. Do you want to live with someone who keeps his nose to the grindstone on weeknights or someone who bumps and grinds to disco music during the optimal study hours?

Sometimes the off campus housing office will make an effort to counter the impersonality of the forms and computer printouts by hosting an open house. At U. Va., Mary told us that such gatherings are more like parties with drinks and munchies. The woman who runs that office distributes name tags. Sharers get ones with a picture of a house on them; seekers get blank name tags. Then the seekers cluster around the sharers and ply them with admirable stories about themselves. Said Mary, "It's kind of like a blind-date convention. You may be frustrated if you come away without housemates, but I had one friend who found a house and *six* housemates at one of them!"

A Roommate Referral Service: Close Up

Small Fee. Conversation Free. By their discreet ad concealed in the "House to Share" classifieds of *The Washington Post*, you would hardly know what Roommates Preferred is all about. Any one of their devoted clientele will be quick to tell you that it happens to be the Washington, D.C., area's most preferred roommate referral service of the five or six that have sprung up since group housing became a viable option in the 1970s.

Synonymous with Roommates Preferred is Betsy Neal, the heart and soul of the business. She looks as unpretentious as the comfy basement apartment she operates from, but don't let her gentle, laid-back appearance fool you. She is constantly alert to every word, gesture, and look you give. It's as if she has antennas out to plumb the depths of a stranger's character, often before a word is spoken. For the past eight years, she has been doing just that for a living.

Betsy started Roommates Preferred in 1974 with David Anderson, her low-profile partner, who does all the behind-the-scenes office management. They took over an older service, Roommate Referral, begun in 1964 by Jeanne Harris, who, Betsy says, "... pioneered the concept of shared resident referral. Seeing the potential for such a service and realizing the gross mismanagement of Roommate Referral, we decided to begin our own service. We thought roommates would be a good little business," she laughs. "The thing just mushroomed. We started before there were even co-ed houses—prehistoric times." David, ever ready with facts and figures, adds, "And we've averaged between fifteen and twenty percent growth per year, serving about 1,500 to 2,000 people a year!"

The success of their service, they both concede, has been due in large part to the failing economy. As it gets worse and more people can't afford to live alone, business for them ironically gets better. Still, the failing economy cannot begin to explain the success of their particular service compared to the others in D.C. Their popularity rests on the unique way they do business and on Betsy's personality—neither of which can be taken separately. They run, as another ad line promises, a "service of trust."

We work very differently from other services. See, all the other services let you register over the telephone. All you have to do is give them your credit card number or send in a check and tell them your preferences over the phone. Anyone can say anything over the telephone, but it's tough to sit right across a desk and talk, looking each other straight in the eye. So, everyone comes in. It gives me a chance to get to know the people better, and it makes them put out a little effort. It also screens out the undesirables.

This initial meeting fulfills the "conversation free" promise in their ad. It *is* more like a rambling conversation than an interview. During it, prospective clients tell Betsy about their preferences while she scribbles down the vital statistics and comments on a form (blue for people seeking housing and yellow for people seeking housemates). Often these meetings turn into "shrink sessions" or talks on all sorts of non-roommate topics. If the client decides Betsy can help, then he or she registers by paying a $30 fee and signing a contract.

The contract and slightly higher fee are other features that separate Roommates Preferred from competing services. The contract outlines the terms of the agreement, like the basically non-refundable fee, which remains good until the client finds a living situation through Roommates Preferred. If clients find housing or housemates from another source, then they are free to use the service at a later time without paying again. If within sixty days the new arrangement is just not working out, only then is the fee refunded.

Coming in for an interview, signing a contract, and paying slightly more than you would for another service may seem like too much to go through for a list of names and numbers that may not materialize into housemates. But Betsy maintains that Roommates Preferred also shows trust by doing something virtually unheard of in these days when people are prone to remark, I've just got my VISA card. I'm a real person now. Roommates Preferred does not accept credit cards for payment, only personal checks (no I.D.s needed) or cash. "If people aren't who they say they are," explained David, "then they've got problems. Either you have enough money to pay the rent or you don't. That's between you and prospective housemates. If the check isn't good, it's going to bounce, and then you've got to deal with Betsy."

"Dealing with Betsy" is what finally makes people put their fate and faith in Roommates Preferred's voluminous accordian files. "The genius of the roommating is Betsy," David says. "If each person has a perfect job in their life, well, Betsy's found hers. For her personality and her emotional/mental makeup and background, this is just the perfect job." She is like a master jigsaw puzzle artist connecting people instead of puzzle pieces, sometimes finding housing for whole offices. Once she found group houses for the whole tympany section of the National Symphony Orchestra. What really excites her is each individual person. "There have been people who, when they first came in, were real shy, just wanting to live with one other person," explains Betsy. "The next time it's with three people, the next time into a co-op, and five or six years later, they're head of a household."

However talented Betsy is at her modern day matchmaking, it's still hard work and long hours: six days a week from 8:30 a.m. to as late as 9:30 p.m. David claims that roommating just can't be done right on a hired basis. They tried to hire others, but it was disastrous. "You have to *love* it," he says. And you can hear that love in Betsy's voice when she picks up the telephone, "Hi! Hey, I'm glad you called. Listen, I've found a place you'd really like."

Is a roommate referral service for *You*?

If you're a sharer, it's almost silly not to make use of a reputable roommate referral service, since all you stand to lose is about $5 each when you split the fee five ways. For seekers who have to foot the fee themselves, it's not a spur of the moment decision. As either a sharer or seeker, you also have to consider the time it takes to find housemates when using a service as your main source. Though Roommates Preferred says "finding time" averages ten days, it will vary from service to service and generally takes longer than using notices, because of the constant telephoning and screening performed by both the service and yourself. So you should never stop hunting for housemates or households through other sources.

Money and time aside, the reputation of any roommate service you might use bears looking into. You find people running them purely to make fast cash, since starting and running a service involves very little capital outlay. All one needs is a place to make calls, a phone, and a filing system. Be smart and do some investigative work before you fork over your money. First "let your fingers do the walking through the yellow pages" of the phone book. If a service is listed there, then you know it has been in business for at least six months. You can also do more extensive detective work by calling the local Better Business Bureau or your Chamber of Commerce.

Once on the telephone, pay attention to the person's voice for signs of a too casual or a brisk, impersonal attitude. Be wary if they start asking you questions about things that are none of their business, like sexual habits or how much money you make. No matter how they sound or what they say, *do not pay in advance or register over the telephone.* Go see them first. Check out the location of their office. Is it a newly renovated part of town or a section that has gone to seed? Just as it's important to know whether a roommate service has been in business long, it's important to see whether they conduct business as if they want to stay in business for more than a short "take-the-money-and-run" summer stint.

If you live in a large city like New York or if you have specific preferences for housemates, you should ask around to find out what type of clientele a particular service favors. Roommates Preferred, for instance, serves college-educated professionals. Another service in Washington places only women, another only gays, and yet another only Christians. Some services sponsor singles get-togethers on weekends, and a service in Boston hosts discussion forums on topics pertinent to group house life.

Most important of all when you use a roommate referral service, remember that you can't expect any more than leads to potential houses or housemates. The following up, telephone screening, interviewing, and getting alone once you decide you have a match made is *up to you.*

Appendix I is a directory of Roommate Referral Services around the country.

The First Connection: Telephone Screening

The more screening you do through the paper, notices, and other sources, the better. But don't worry even if you've just done the minimum. You've got two more steps to go in the housemate selection process: screening over the telephone and through the interview.

The first time sharers and seekers talk on the phone may be the last, or to quote Humphrey Bogart, it "... could be the beginning of a very beautiful friendship." Approaches to this important initial contact vary from house to house. Some sharers opt for intensive telephone screening, searching for a good connection over the wires in more ways than one. Jim is a member of such a household:

> *One thing we look for is whether people are comfortable with lesbians and gay men. We screen for this over the phone and not on our sign, since we don't want people dropping by out of curiosity . . . our last pre-interview screening was great. We made a whole list of what was important to us. My first conversation*

with Ellen lasted at least a half hour. She asked me
lots of questions, and I asked her lots of questions.

Other sharers favor a more businesslike approach to telephone screening. They dispense with questions like, What are you interested in? What do you do? Or the infamous, What's your major? They inquire instead about stances on more clear-cut issues: Do you smoke? Do you want to share food and cooking? How do you feel about pets? A screening on basic issues only is often a necessity for sharers who find themselves inundated with calls. Both sharers and seekers would be wise to keep a list of all their questions, whether on sexual preferences or smoking, by the telephone. Ian, a young and impressionable man who lived in a group house during his internship in a congressional office, remembers talking at length with a prospective housemate but forgetting to state one crucial question, Do you mind sharing a house with two cats? It turned out that the woman, with whom he felt immediately in sync, was allergic to cats, something he didn't find out until she started sneezing uncontrollably three minutes in-to the interview. After that incident, Ian's house made up a "topics for discussion" list to post by the kitchen phone.

At the very least, telephone screening can eliminate undesirables. Said Jim of his house's last attempt to fill a vacancy:

We had our share of strange people. Someone called
up, and she sounded nice, interesting, and practical.
Then she mentioned that she levitated. She went right
into this dream state when she started talking about
levitating. It was too much for us. I mean, she could
have come floating into my room one night.

The Congenial Interview

Some people don't like the word *interview*. They complain

that interviewing conjures up an image of uncomfortable chairs, fluorescent lights, and perspiration. Yet the word *interview* has become as ingrained in group house "culture" as the words *group house* are for describing a shared living arrangement among three or more people. Besides, *interview* literally describes a mutual looking over. So take the interview out of the office, and put it in the battered but comfy living room of a group house. It takes on a much more inviting aura. On what other occasion will you be able to entertain total strangers or enter strange houses to be plied with beer, pretzels, fascinating personalities, and a guided tour of the "grounds"?

Interviews can take all forms. They can be haphazard, as in Steve's house:

> *There was no interviewing. I just came one night. Heidi was watching a ballet on T.V. and couldn't care less. I just showed myself around the house. I had no experience with group house living. The rooms were nice. She seemed okay though preoccupied. It seemed like it would be tolerable. Plus, she mentioned that people were moving out so I knew I'd have some input.*

Interviews can be orderly, set up like a doctor's appointment with seekers scheduled in half-our slots. There are open houses where sharers ask all who are interested to show up at the same time. Since sharers usually set the tone for the whole interview, there are ways in which they can conduct it to minimize hassle and make the whole affair less intimidating and chaotic for seekers.

Interviewing Tips For Sharers

Some households prefer to have the person who is moving out arrange and conduct the interviews. They reason that this person should do penance for causing them the inconvenience of losing a housemate. Actually, it's a terrible way to find new housemates. *You*, not the departing housemate, will have to live with the new person. So say farewell to old housemates and figure out who, among those remaining, will be on hand to interview prospective members.

Setting aside a weekend or day for interviewing and getting all of your housemates to be there is actually more of a task than the interviewing itself. It's important that everyone meet prospective housemates, but you can assign the preliminary interviewing to selected members. The rest of you can congregate later to meet the two or three finalists. Interviewing people for vacancies in your group house is, after all, a little like hosting a Miss America Pageant. If you've agreed on what type of person you want in your house, then you should be able to trust housemates to pick promising people out of the crowd.

As for the *how* of interviewing, four out of five seekers favor the doctor's office method—each interviewee gets some time alone with house members. "One-on-one is vital for a group house," said Barry, who spent the better part of a month seeking housing. "Group interviews are disgusting!" Unfortunately, many sharers prefer interviewing en masse. They think that this "formal chaos," as Barry dubbed the group interview, is less time-consuming than the one-on-one approach. Such sharers are probably hurting themselves as well as the hopefuls who sit packed in their living room, each trying to outshine the other. With the rent overdue for the unfilled room, it's hard to remember that your prime objective is to find compatible housemates, not to save time, and therefore, money. Think of the long run and how much you'd stand to lose if your hastily selected housemate turns out to be a bad choice. Furthermore, if you have such a large field that the group interview seems to be the only solution, you are probably using the wrong sources or not screening thoroughly on the telephone.

To interview as many people as possible and still allow everyone a personal interview, you can do what one house did with the uncanny smoothness of an assembly line. They set up the first interview for 10:00 a.m. and subsequent interviews at fifteen-minute intervals. The first person got the tour of the house (given by all housemates) from 10:00 to 10:15 and while he was in the living room chatting with half of the housemates, the others gave the next person the tour and "pitch." At 10:30, the first interviewee left, the second was down in the living room chatting with those who didn't give the tour, and the rest of the housemates were opening the door for the third interviewee. In effect, the bases are loaded and everything will go smoothly until somebody hits an unexpected pop fly by coming too late or too early. Also, having interviews back-to-back like this doesn't allow you any time to discuss candidates with your housemates after they leave—the only instance in group living when talking behind someone's back is condoned! Run people through the interview mill too quickly, and your impressions get diffuse as you are called upon later to pick out the most compatible ones.

Although this house's timing of the interviews left a little to be desired, their procedures made good sense. By giving a tour of the house first, they gave some much-needed direction to those first awkward moments when seeker and sharer meet. By the time the tour was over, the fog of tension had lifted sufficiently for everyone to relax, be themselves, and get to the heart of the group house interview.

On the Couch: Group House Talk Show

When seeker and sharer are face to face, whether on the couch, at the dining room table, or leaning up against a wall, it's time to form impressions and opinions of each other. This is definitely one area of life in which your gut impressions are of paramount importance. *You just can't live with someone you feel the slightest bit queasy about.*

For some, this period of "feeling each other out" (in more progressive houses this phrase is taken quite literally) is very informal. For example, Leo, the undisputed leader of his all male household in Dallas, said, "After I gave the pitch, we just sat down together in the living room, cracked a few beers, and started talking."

When your time is limited, however, it's best for sharers to give the proceedings some semblance of order. Denise spoke of her house's process of refining their interview technique:

> *At first we just sat around and talked, but we realized that we had to develop questions about things that were important. Otherwise, it tended to go off on all tangents. We got it down to a formula. We went around and said what we were doing with our lives and what our primary interest was. That took about an hour, and the person never got to say anything! So, we had to condense that. We gave them a chance to talk and say what was important, and then we would usually have a question and answer period.*

The members of Denise's house finally realized how easy it is to get derailed during an interview, rambling on to points of conversation that have nothing to offer for the task at hand: finding out if you can live with each other. Seekers, in particular, can get frustrated, since they are at the mercy of the sharers during the interview. Use the interview checklist, with your own additions, to keep the ad hoc chatter on track.

Tour Checklist for Seekers

☐ Look at the condition of the house. Is it messy, dimly lit? Does it look comfortable, like people really live there?

☐ Inspect the kitchen, and ask to see the inside of the refrigerator—as good a gauge as any to the concern or lack thereof about house cleanliness. Trashcans are also indicative of cleaning standards. Does it look like the trash hasn't been taken out for weeks? Or worse yet, has it been hidden on the porch, behind a door?!

☐ Find out how many bathrooms there are, and ask to see all of them. If you're fond of baths, check for layers of footprints in the tub. If you're a shower type, ask about water pressure and whether there is any problem with crowding in the morning.

☐ Check out how the house is heated or cooled. What does the average monthly utility bill come to?

☐ See the room for rent, get its rough dimensions, and note whether it can take a double bed, stereo, et cetera. Is there a closet? Many older houses lack them. What is the view like? Is your prospective bedroom hotter or colder than others? Does it face North or South? Does it get the morning sun?

☐ Visit the other bedrooms. If they differ in size, ask how they're pro-rated and who gets the bigger rooms.

☐ Venture down to the basement. Is there a washer and dryer? If not, ask about the local laundromat situation. Also, find out about storage space, for your bike, luggage, artwork, whatever.

☐ Child-check the house if you have children. Do the housemates keep sharp objects lying about? Is there "artwork" hanging up that you wouldn't feel comfortable exposing your child to?

☐ View the yard. Find out what the neighbors and neighborhood are like.

☐ Look over the physical appearance and upkeep of the house. Is the ceiling cracked and about to cave in? Are there any leaks? Asking about house maintenance can lead directly to the question of whether the landlord is prompt about upkeep and repair.

☐ Add your own criteria here.

_____

_____

_____

_____

_____

_____

_____

_____

Interview checklist for Seekers

☐ Do you feel comfortable with the housemates? This doesn't mean you should only think of moving into a group house if you immediately feel relaxed when you first meet your housemates, but the more you feel you can be yourself, the better.

☐ Try to get a feel not just for how you relate to individual members of the house but how they relate to each other.

☐ How cohesive is the house? How long have they known each other? Are some people in the house really buddy-buddy? You might ask how they got together. While you're at it, why did the last person leave?

☐ Find out about the mechanics of the house. If sharing food is a necessity for you, you probably screened for food sharers over the phone, but you might ask how they divide the food bill. If cleaning is a concern to you, ask if they have a schedule. Find out what the bottom level of interaction is, and how much do they interact beyond that. Are there regular house meetings?

☐ Ask about the lease. Is there one? How long does it run? Would you have to sign it? How often do people move in and out? Or how stable is the house? Is it just a place to live, a semi-permanent living situation, or somewhere in between?

☐ Use this space to write down any other concerns you'd like to discuss before you are in the interview.

_____

_____

_____

_____

As long as you are thinking about things you *should* do, here are a few things that will certainly turn off prospective housemates during the all-important interview.

Name That Idiosyncracy—Interview Don'ts

Don'ts For Seekers:

Don't talk about how many interviews you've been through that day, week, or month. If you do, you'll get tossed from interview to interview like a hot potato. Never let those interviewing you sniff a whiff of desperation.

Don't bring offerings of banana bread, wine, chocolate cookies—in short, don't bribe sharers. Offer to cook for them *after* you move in.

Don't bring your resume to an interview. It *really* happens in these career-conscious times, but it jars with the informal style of most group houses.

Don'ts For Sharers:

Don't ask trick questions during the interview. Suzy, who interviews prospective housemates at least once every three months in her transient household of six told us how annoying this is. "Dennis asks people all the time, and he just thinks he's clever if they have any idiosyncracies. I think that's more a test of wit than a real test of their personality. A person who scores high on that will pass Dennis's test. It's always such a relief to me when somebody I like can pull through that!"

Don't be too general. Another man complained that in one house, members sat sprawled on the couch facing him and without any preamble a woman glared at him intensely and said, "Tell us about yourself." Come *on.* That approach bombs on a first date and bombs during a group house interview.

"Adequate with All Illusions Gone"—Making the Big Decision

Interviewing and being interviewed, as you may have guessed, is an exhausting process. By now you may be wondering when to stop. In the seeker's case, the answer is sadly obvious: you don't until you are accepted into a house that suits you. You may have decided "that's it" about the last house you visited; they may have decided "he's the one" about the person who visited the day after you did. If you're a sharer, you should stop interviewing after you and your housemates have found three people you can live with.

During the interview process, you'll accrue vast stores of information about everyone you talk to, and the facts and impressions that belong to each candidate fast become foggy unless you develop a method of distinguishing among people or households. In addition to discussing each person with housemates, sharers should keep a notebook of file cards with each seeker's name and number listed above a space for comments. Comments can be cryptic (braids, punk glasses, transcriber, loves cats) or in-depth personality profiles.

Seekers would be wise to keep records as well. Paul, a meticulous law student who keeps detailed records on various aspects of his life in an accordian file, said that he kept an index card on each house that interviewed him. When it came time to make a fast decision between two houses, he had in front of him the pros and cons of each, neatly outlined. He laughed when he found the card he had written on his present group house. It said simply, "adequate with all illusions gone."

Who knows? In the near future when everyone has their own computer terminal, you may be able to feed all your notes to the computer and ... Voila! Your perfectly matched housemate will flash onto the screen. For the present, you must do the compatibility computation yourself. Sometimes you'll be lucky enough to experience group house "love at first sight." Phil, a "rookie" at interviewing but not at group house living, had previously booked rooms to friends. He was lucky on his house's first round of interviews:

We didn't have a line of questions. We just dealt with each person spontaneously and tried to get impressions and talked about our impressions after each person left. Generally speaking, it was always clear as soon as they stepped out the door that we were not particularly interested in that person, and then David came bouncing in. One of the women wasn't there, so it was me and the other woman in that situation. The minute he walked out of the room we both looked at each other and said, "Yes, no question." When the other housemate came, we told her about this fellow, and she said she felt she needed to meet him before she could agree. So then he arranged to come by and see us. It was out of his way since he was on his way out of town, and it was also a very costly thing to do. Cheerfully he bounced into the room, spent five minutes with us, and the minute he left, we looked at this woman, and she said, "You're absolutely right, he's the one."

Everyone has his or her own test that a prospective housemate must pass before deciding, yes, that person is the one. While in Phil's house, David spontaneously passed everyone's tests, don't expect that to happen in your house. Most households report that the only way to make sure a prospective housemate is o.k. with everyone is to use a minority veto or the consensus process in which each house member must agree before a course of action is taken. You can vote on whether to get cable television or to cook on Saturdays instead of Fridays, but the issue of who you are going to share your living space with is infinitely more sensitive. It's simple but not always clear: Nobody should have to live with somebody, *whatever the reasons*—that you don't want to should be reason enough. Remember, you should discuss a "runner up" in case the person you first choose doesn't choose your house.

Seekers have to make their decision alone, and those who have been househunting for a long time might feel like they have no choice. If you start to think that way, a danger sign should flash in your head. You do have a choice; you can always find a place to stay in an emergency. Your choice is just more limited. Or you may be choosing between two places and will probably have to make your decision fast.

Decision Tie-Breakers

If you aren't clear about which house you'd like to join, here are some points to consider that will help seekers and sharers alike make the big decision.

Not only who you live with but how many people you live with can greatly determine how happy you are in a group house. Three is generally an unlucky number in group living. Why? Inevitably two become closer and the third feels like exactly that, a third party constantly watching from the outside. It can be even more unpleasant when two gang up on one. Ed relates, "The main thing the two of us had in common was our extreme dislike of this other person." You can imagine how awful it would be to be that *other person*. Usually, the only time living in threes becomes workable is when the odd one out is someone seeking an arrangement that enables him to live cheaply but obscurely. A case in point is nineteen-year-old George, who lives with Marianne and Steven, a couple in their late twenties:

> *The atmosphere in our house has been good. The real*
> *bonus in this arrangement for me is that Marianne and*
> *Steven are lovers. If there are three people in one*
> *place and two are very concentrated on each other, it*

diverts scrutiny on the third party. And if there is anything that has kept this house working well, it is that there hasn't been a lot of scrutiny on myself. I think anyone's hard to live with, but I think I'm very hard to live with. I'm impressionable right now. They listen to me, but there's a point where they say, 'shut up," and go off into their room.

Add a fourth person to a group of three, and you come into the ideal range of four to six people. In a group of five, for instance, you can become very close to one or two members and keep your distance from another hard-to-live-with member. Be cautious about going beyond six housemates. "There's anonymity already with six. You don't know who's making the dirt," complained one "Felix Unger" divorcé who had to dramatically readjust his cleaning standards when he moved in with five others. Remember, agreeing on important house issues with eight other people is nearly impossible, if not totally exhausting. Last, but certainly not least, you should check out the bathroom situation if you are considering joining a large household. It won't be untoward of you to put "bathroom schedule" on your list of interview topics if there are only two bathrooms.

When you know you want to live in a co-ed house, try to get into a house or form one that has an equal (or near-equal) ratio of men and women. Group house dwellers speak often of a "balance between male and female energies" that can be crucial to the atmosphere of a co-ed house. This balance may show in the things you take for granted when you're living with men and women. One man is constantly delighted that there are always fresh flowers in his house. They almost became a given to him until Jenny, the secret flower arranger, was gone for a weekend, and the vases stood empty with petals from past bouquets heaped forlornly around them. Then there's Wendy who has a late night accounting class only a few blocks away from her group house. To walk those few blocks alone would mean enticing muggers and rapists. So every Thursday night one of her three male housemates is there to meet her and walk her home.

Imagine, if Wendy lived in a house with all other women except for one man, then the man might start to feel put upon by his masculine duties. Going back to the threesome of George, Marianne and Steven, Marianne does at least ninety percent of the cleaning. This suits George and Steven just fine, and George says nonchalantly, "If the arrangement bothers her, I haven't heard any noises about it." But perhaps Marianne is fuming inside, "If I do just one more dish . . . !" If you are a seeker, don't put yourself into a position where you are a minority of one as far as equality between the sexes goes, and if you're a sharer, try to avoid creating that situation.

Don't look at a prospective housemate as a prospective lover. Chapter 5 deals with the hazards of in-house affairs in some detail. Suffice it to say that if you partake of an in-house amour you are setting yourself up for an extremely volatile situation both in your house and in the relationship because the two cannot be separated. If you feel that tug of desire inside, be forewarned—get the person's number for a future rendezvous, and go on to set up your next interview.

You might have in mind an ideal age range for your prospective housemate, but try not to be an "ageist." Many people who say they prefer housemates over twenty-five are simply trying to draw a line between students and professionals. Keep your mind open, at least a crack, because often someone who is twenty-three may show as much maturity as someone thirty-three. On the other hand, parents contemplating group living have good reason for being "ageists" because they have to consider the environment they are providing for their children. If you are trying to get into a house that requires you to be within a certain age range and you don't qualify, always be honest about it—if you lie and are found out later, you housemates will take that act as a true sign of immaturity.

Things can be bought, but good housemates can't. "Hi, Jane, well I just called to tell you we'd like you to move in with us . . . great, you can! Hey, listen, you *are* bringing your T.V. and toaster oven aren't you? . . Great, we can't wait for them . . . I mean *you.*" This welcoming message from her future housemates, Gail and Joanne, should have warned Jane that she was heading for disaster, but she was relieved to have found "a place to live." She waived her niggling doubts that Gail and Joanne were more interested in her appliances than her, moved in, and moved out three months later. Nor should seekers move into a house solely because it is beautiful, without regard for the housemates. Sally, a paralegal in Washington, D.C., and a first-time house hunter, remembers falling in love with the first house she saw. When it came time to talk with its members, "I noticed that they kept making sarcastic jabs at each other. I think it was in good humor, but I was sure I didn't want to live with people who I never knew if they really meant anything they said. . . even to have lived in that gorgeous house."

Above all, pay attention to your gut impression when deciding who to live with. If you feel inside that "he's the one," then go with the feeling, even to the extent that you have to disregard some of the other points just outlined.

The Etiquette of Accepting and Rejecting

Accepting a housemate or house and rejecting the same can be a sticky business. Since Emily Post was writing well before the dawn of the group house as we know it, here are some general guidelines to help unstick you.

Sharers shouldn't find the task of accepting too burdensome. Remember to have at least three people lined up as possible housemates, because the person you picked may have chosen another group house. If the lucky person would like to have a few days to consider your invitation, respect that, but set a time limit, say a week, after which you will fill the space with someone else. Smart sharers, who want to ease the hassle of being housemateless in the event that a new housemate bows out after saying yes, request a $50 down payment upon acceptance. It reserves the space for the new person and keeps the sharers solvent if they are forced to find another housemate when the rent is past due.

Many seekers think nothing of saying yes to one house, scouting around for a still better situation, and then backing out of the first agreement. They figure that they are put at a disadvantage during the whole interview process and it's time to turn the tables on those who have the advantage of housing. It is tempting to do this, especially when you've been discouraged by fruitless interviews and suddenly three houses want you. But even though you may not see face to face the people you disappoint (anger is actually more like it), you have to realize that once you move into a house you may be put in the same position sometime in the future. Also, living successfully in a group house involves thinking of the advantages and repercussions of your actions for everyone. If you have a blind, me-first vision, then perhaps a group house is not for you. So, if you are deciding between two or more places, *stall for time*. One last word about accepting: find out the date of your big move so you can avoid any confusion.

How does a sharer go about telling all those names and all those faces behind the names that, alas, the house has found someone else? Some find the task so disagreeable that they lose all names and numbers "accidentally on purpose." Because of the transient nature of most groups, today's sharers could be tomorrow's seekers. So, why give a bunch of homeless people insomnia? Divide up the list of unfortunates and have everyone in your house call four or five. All you have to say is, "I'm sorry, but we found someone else to live here." When an adamant seeker demands to know, as if to gain insight for the next interview, lie if you have to because, in this instance, what you do know might hurt you. Sheree handled it this way:

> *We tried to call the rejected people back. To the men, I said that we took a woman, which was easy, but wasn't an answer. And to the women I said that we met a lot of people we really liked and —I tried to make it as*

nice as possible—that we decided to take somebody else who said she could move in before you would be available.

No matter what is said over the telephone, rejection hurts and is probably the most wearing and discouraging part of the whole interview process. You see a dozen places, get your hopes up about five of them, and diligently follow each one up with phone calls. Sometimes you get a flat, No, we've filled the spot. Sometimes you get an, I'll call you, and they don't, leaving you in an agony of suspense, not to mention a real bind. Don't take this rejection personally. You have no way of knowing the circumstances that led up to each no. If you do start taking each rejection as a personal affront, then it begins to show when you go to the next interview and the next. Nobody wants to live with someone who comes off as a loser. *Be as upbeat as possible,* even if you've been looking for a month or your present housemates are about to throw your things in the street.

Transition Time: The Big Move

Once the happy task of accepting the chosen housemate and the chore of rejecting the unchosen are over, sharers should attend to making the transition from old housemate to new. During this time, groups often feel suspended between "goodbye" and "welcome." One way to settle your household back onto its foundations is to make sure that the financial obligations of old and new housemates are clear to everyone. In the next chapter, you'll find advice on how to handle the passage of security deposit monies in a way that even solves the problem of leftover bills. You should also be clear about arrival and departure dates. This information is important, especially when the new housemate moves in mid-month, so that accurate financial records can be kept. Furthermore, specifying the exact moving dates for both the incoming and outgoing housemate can prevent a disaster: There's a knock on the front door at 11:30 one Saturday morning just as two of six housemates are straggling out of bed. Your new housemate is standing on the steps looking very awake, having just parked her rent-a-truck in the driveway. You'd be delighted to see her, except for the fact that the housemate she's replacing is still upstairs sleeping in her "not-to-be-moved-until-next-week" bed. *Somebody* screwed up the dates. . . . Meanwhile, where do you put a rent-a-truck?

Moving day is always a memorable experience in group house life. Andy remembered how surprised he was when he moved into his house in Philadelphia before his first semester at Temple University:

> *I was amazed how my housemates fixed the room up—which hadn't looked at all promising when I first saw it! They set up the twin bed with a little night table by it, and they loaned me a huge dresser as well. My new house key was on the bed with a big ribbon around it and a card that said, WELCOME HOME.*

Jackie, a researcher at M.I.T. in Cambridge, remembers her moving day with less nostalgia than Andy. She and her mother carried a hefty double bed up three flights of stairs while Arthur, the only housemate at home, sat downstairs watching T.V., oblivious to their intermittent grunting, sighing, and banging. "After my mom and I practically stumbled back down the stairs," she says with some residual anger in her voice, "Arthur hopped up from the Lazy-boy chair and said, 'Hey, could you use some help?' "

You don't have to take as many pains as Andy's housemates did when he moved in, but you will start out on the right foot if eveyone lifts a finger. As with any group house chore, the work will seem lighter if you make moving day into a party. Have a big house dinner afterwards as a way to welcome the new housemate.

For their part, newcomers can become more at ease mainly by being themselves, but not trying to force intimacy with house members. When you enter a group house, you have to realize that the existing balance among the housemates has been temporarily disrupted. You may be replacing a sorely missed house member or somebody who soured the group feeling by leaving in an inconsiderate rush. Eva remembers moving into her house, which she's lived in now for one year, and trying hard to break into the seeming clique of the three established housemates:

> *The more I tried to be part of the group, the more I felt rejected by them—as if they thought I was being presumptuous. Then one of them, Lorraine, and I got to know each other gradually, and it was through our tentative friendship that I felt myself being drawn into the warmth of the tight little circle. Now it's hard to imagine ever feeling like the outsider. Yet it made me very careful about not excluding the woman who moved in after Lorraine left.*

As the newcomer, you'd do well to reconcile yourself to spending some time sitting it out and waiting for your turn to cut in on the group's intricate house "dance" pattern. Then again, you may be as fortunate as the two newest members in Lucy's house:

> *These two men were amazingly quick at getting into the house jokes—which is often the most difficult thing to do when moving into an established household. Even though one is extremely shy and the other rather loud, they both, in some way, became accomplices instead of outsiders watching at the window.*

Advanced Group Living:
Scene 1. The Big Party

"After we lived in the house for about two months and got to know and like each other, we decided to have a party. It wasn't what you call a formal group decision, we never had house meetings. There was just a sort of a ground swell of interest.

"I think Julie and I planted the seed. We had seven people in the house. Julie and I were sitting around talking one night when it dawned on us that if we each invited twenty people we'd have a guest list of 140 people.

"So we floated the idea, and everyone got excited, so excited that we managed to schedule the one and only house meeting we ever had to plan the party. At the meeting, the first order of business was to select a Saturday night when everyone would be in town. That took some doing, but we finally settled on a date about five weeks away, the weekend before the Memorial Day holiday. We knew the weather would probably be great, and it left plenty of time to spread the word that this was an event not to be missed.

"The next item on the agenda was our budget. I'd thought my housemates were tightwads, so I was amazed when everyone agreed to kick in $40. That gave us $280, which seems like a lot but isn't much for 150 people. So we decided to encourage people to B.Y.O.B. as well.

"Then we started spreading the word. Before we knew it, the list of people who said they were coming was up to 175.

"Tom and I were nominated to make a party tape. We had three big common rooms on the ground floor of the house, and we decided to clear every last piece of furniture from one room to make a dance floor. We figured we could put Tom's speakers on one side of the room and run the speaker wire out the window and up to a room upstairs.

"Between the seven of us, we had about 600 records. I was a D.J. on my college radio station, and the tape we made was unbelievable—Dionne Warwick, Motown, swing music like Bob Wills and His Texas Playboys, Van Morrison, the Clash, you name it . . .

"Finally, party day arrived. We weren't the tidiest group of people, but the party inspired us to clean up. Julie had a car, so she and Tom went to the liquor store with about $225. They came back with fifteen cases of beer, a good stock of hard liquor, wine, mixers, and ice. We filled a couple of trash cans with ice to chill the beer. We put one on the porch and one in one of the rooms downstairs. At the grocery store we got cups, lemons and limes, and potato chips and other munchies. Another crew worked all day in the kitchen, turning out hundreds of stuffed grape leaves and chocolate chip cookies, dips of every kind, and huge trays of cheese.

"After six, things got quiet. People took naps and showers, and we set up the stereo and played some quiet jazz.

"People started showing up around 9:00. One of the first was a guy carrying an eight millimeter projector and a print of *King Kong*. We let him set up in one of the bedrooms and put up some signs around the house advertising the movie upstairs.

"The flood started around 10:30. It seemed like there was a constant stream of people coming in the door. I guess about sixty percent of them were total strangers to me, but I picked out a few I definitely wanted to meet. Then at about 11:30 we got to the hard-driving part of the dance tape. It felt like the building was shaking. The dance room was becoming a sauna bath, but the porch was nice and cool and pretty quiet.

"I wandered around the house. People were sitting on the stairs and standing on the landing talking. A few of my housemates took their friends into the quiet of their rooms, but even some of their stereos were going. In the movie room, old *Popeye* cartoons were being shown as a preview to the second run of *King Kong*. There was a generalized feeling of anarchy permeating the house.

"The party went on at this incredible pitch of activity until about 2:30. The crowd started to dwindle, but the last people who did leave left around 4:00. A few people, if you know what I mean, didn't leave until the next day.

"I met a lot of new people at the party. Even a couple of people I knew in college came who I didn't know were in town. It turned out they worked with one of my housemates.

"In retrospect, it was the high point of the two years I spent in that house. For a lot of reasons. Everyone in the house really pulled together to bring it off, and it was a real success. A lot of people called, and I ran into a lot of people on the street who told me they had a really great time. There were probably 120 people for me to meet. And we were mostly in our early twenties, still young enough to party with abandon.

"A lot of future dinner parties were spin-offs from our big party. A lot of good will and new friendships were generated and that momentum went way beyond the party.

"I was new to town. I would have gone crazy living alone in an apartment and seeing only the people I worked with. I can definitely say that the opportunity to meet new people was the best thing about living in a group house for me."

Laying a Foundation: Group House Organization

There is no doubt that finding the right people to live with is the essential first step in setting up a group house. However, all the screening in the world will not make your house a pleasant place unless everyone has clear expectations of each other and communicates openly about them. Whenever adults get together, there are bound to be differing, even conflicting, expectations about the mechanisms of running a house. If these go unresolved, they can easily lead to strained relations and possibly to the disintegration of the household.

Clarity is the Key

Strain can be caused by something as simple as the definition of a clean bathroom: You call *that* a clean bathroom? You didn't even empty the trash or sweep the floor. Or it could be as complex as friendships within the group: You're never here in the evenings. You don't go out with us any more. What do you mean? I never promised to spend all my spare time at home.

Whatever the actual issue, the solution to the problems it causes is to spend some time thinking about the group and personal expectations. At the very least, the exercise will give you some insight into how and why people differ. Once you understand a person's motives, you can be, perhaps, a bit more tolerant about living with him or her.

While you are giving some thought to expectations, potential sources of friction that you and your housemates should consider are:

- How long are members expected to stay in the house? One year? Two years? six months?
- What are the standards for cleanliness and order in the house?
- Which food system will be appropriate for your group? Will it accomodate people's diets?
- How should common space and possessions be used?
- What are the financial arrangements and responsibilities?
- How should major decisions be made?
- Are there any rules governing sex in the house? Are couples welcome? Are lovers welcome? Should you have a "no-incest rule" among housemates?
- Should drugs or other illegal substances be allowed in the house?

- Is there a limit to how long guests can stay? Should they be asked to contribute to household finances?
- How do you feel about smoking? Permit it everywhere? Only in the bedrooms? Not in the kitchen? Not at all?
- Are children welcome? Are pets allowed? Who takes responsibility for children, pets, and plants?

All of these issues are discussed further in Chapters 4 or 5.

In an effort to define the type of house you have created and what is expected of each member, it may be helpful for you to write a house profile, a brief description of the arrangements and systems that can be changed as needed. Use the profile from 3319 16th Street (Example 3.1) as a guide to develop your own.

Example 3.1: A Sample Group House Profile

3319 16th St. is a group house of not more than seven people who live together for economic convenience and because they basically enjoy each other's company.

The housemates buy food separately and may or may not eat dinner together, whatever seems appropriate and convenient.

Although there is no great emphasis on togetherness, people are expected to be friendly and considerate of each other.

Each member of the house is expected to pick a chore and make sure it gets done at least once every two weeks.

People are expected to pay bills on time or pay any late fees themselves.

Visitors are welcome and so is their money, although it is not demanded.

Cats are the sole responsibility of their owner, Wendy. When Wendy goes, they go.

If you don't want other people to use your things, keep them in your room.

Finally, all housemates are expected to contribute time, money, and enthusiasm to the semi-annual house parties.

If you're in a group that is considering incorporating or becoming a more formal legal entity, you might find an actual constitution appropriate. Example 3.2 is an agreement one group drew up to guide their house life.

Example 3.2: A Sample Group House Constitution

We, the undersigned residents of 717 Smedley Street, have come together to live for a number of reasons. Some of those reasons are:

(1) To live more cheaply by pooling our resources;

(2) To live comfortably by sharing the burdens of house maintenance; and

(3) To live happily by bringing to the house an attitude of cooperation and friendship.

In order to achieve these goals we have made the following agreement.

House Coordinator. The role of the House Coordinator is to handle house accounts and to lead house meetings. The position will rotate alphabetically through the household. The term of the position, which cannot be refused, is one month.

House Meetings. House dinner-meetings will be held on the first and third Wednesdays of each month. We recognize that house meetings are an extremely important part of successful group living and agree to give attendance at house meetings priority over our other activities.

The purposes of the house meeting are to provide a forum for airing grievances and a time to make decisions concerning the house, especially about money and new housemates.

All decisions will be made on a consensus basis.

Finances. All members of the house will be cosigners of the house account. On the first day of each month, each house member will write a check made out to the House Coordinator. The combined amount of the checks will be sufficient to bring the balance in the house accounts to $1500. From the house accounts, rent and utilities will be paid, food will be bought, and other incidental expenses will be met.

The House Coordinator will keep accurate records and will report on finances at the second house meeting of each month.

Food. Food will be bought cooperatively but consumed individually. The only exceptions are the semi-monthly house dinner-meetings. For those meetings, the House Coordinator will cook the meal.

Chores. Chores will be delegated by a work wheel posted in the kitchen. The term for chores will be one month. The five chores will be: (1) House Coordinator; (2) grocery shopping and cleaning the kitchen; (3) cleaning the bathrooms; (4) cleaning the halls, stairs, and common areas; and (5) taking out the trash and exterior maintenance.

Visitors. Each house member may have fourteen free "overnight guest units" each year. Beyond that, housemates may have an overnight guest for each night they spend away from the house.

Expulsion. This is the only exception to the consensus rule. By unanimous vote of the other housemates, a housemate may be asked to leave at the end of the month following the month when the request is made.

Amendments. Changes to this agreement may be made by consensus at any house meeting.

Signed		Date	Departure Date
X	_____	_____	_____
X	_____	_____	_____
X	_____	_____	_____
X	_____	_____	_____
X	_____	_____	_____
X	_____	_____	_____
X	_____	_____	_____

Straight Talk about Group House Communication

Communication, from friendly banter to serious griping, is the lifeblood of any group house and keeps the delicate mechanism of group dynamics running smoothly. It is one of the most important yet most overlooked aspects of a shared lifestyle, a barometer of good will.

Not surprisingly, professional psychiatrists who have studied the so-called urban commune stress the importance of communication among group members. "While it has become a cliche, open communication among commune members was very important to maintaining group cohesion," said Dr. Saul Levine and his colleagues in a paper published in the *American Journal of Orthopsychiatry in 1973.*[2] Their findings hold true for today's group houses as well.

In a group house especially, communication is more than just a courtesy, it is a responsibility. When gripes and worries are out in the open, they can be dealt with. Otherwise, they will fester under the surface, polluting relations among housemates and making life unpleasant for everyone.

The style of communication is every bit as important as the fact that housemates are talking. People who grunt or bang on the walls, people who are unapproachable or whose only form of communication is criticism (You left the light on downstairs. The bathroom was really dirty.) rarely inspire goodwill among their housemates, and often spoil the atmosphere for everyone.

John, a retired government worker who has opened his house to groups for the past twelve years, described the destructive effects of an uncommunicative housemate. "Instead of telling us what was bothering her, she would pout and withdraw and become icy and aloof. She could hold a grudge for days, and that would completely sour and dampen everyone's mood."

In contrast, another member of John's house would let people know immediately about any problems. "If there was some tension, if he were uncomfortable about something, Martin would tell us about it in a strong and stern but kind way. There was never any manipulative game-playing or pouting or punishement."

Chris, who rented a suburban house with two other people, said he knew it was time to move when he found he could no longer talk to one of the women. "The situation was analogous to the problems between the United States and the Soviet Union," he said. "We just couldn't communicate. We'd start out talking and end up snapping at each other. It got so bad that I dreaded going home."

On the other hand, some housemates talk far too much, insisting on pouring every intimate detail of their personal lives into the nearest ear. These people have a way of dominating the kitchen, or living room, or wherever they happen to be. They send people scurrying to their rooms for shelter and can be just as difficult to live with as the ones who only grumble or never say a word. After all, it is important to feel comfortable not only in your bedroom but also in the common spaces, or you might as well live in a boarding house. The trick, as always, is to strike a balance between too little communication on the one hand, and too much on the other. See how many of the common communication types listed in the Guide you can identify in your group house.

Common Group House Communication Types

Grunters never say a recognizable word, let alone a complete sentence, so no one really knows how they feel. They are cousins to the *Mumblers*. Although *Grunters* are not the best conversationalists, they can be fairly easy people to get along with. Just interpret their unintelligible responses in the way that best suits the group's needs.

Ear Benders, also known as *Motor Mouths, Yentas, or Yakkers* (depending on the dialect), will tell you their life story five minutes after moving in. They hang out on the stairway, where they are likely to catch you on your way out. They are also found in the kitchen, skewering people to their seats with their chatter. Many a plate of spaghetti has grown cold due to *Ear Benders*. Another favorite perch is near the bathroom, where they entrap the unsuspecting housemate in conversation while he shifts nervously from foot to foot, desperate for a lull. For all their talk, *Ear Benders* are basically nice people, if only a little insensitive.

Complainers come in two types; the *Whiners* and the *Guilt Mongers*. *Whiners*, though boring, are basically harmless people who are easily defeated by life's little traumas—the broken shoelaces and crackpot phone calls that plague us all from time to time. It is the *Guilt Mongers* you have to watch out for. They are bullies, albeit subtle insidious ones. By complaining, they put you on the defensive, even if you've done nothing wrong. *Guilt Mongers* will announce, for example, that an unwashed fork sat in the sink overnight, that a door was left unlocked, that a stereo was playing too loud. They never confront you directly with their complaints when you can do something about it. Instead, they wait until it is too late to remedy the situation, belatedly flexing their muscle in household matters.

Psycho-babblers while earnest and well meaning, insist on discussing every issue to death. They are likely to call a house meeting over the most trivial matters. Once in the meeting, they play defender to the downtrodden or devil's advocate. These people like to examine their feelings publicly and encourage others to do the same. They might, for example, ask you how you're doing and then insist you're not telling the truth.

Shouters like to carry on conversations with people on the third floor while they are in the living room. They have something important, even private, to tell you while you're in the shower. Rather than walk a flight or two when the telephone rings, these people will scream: Har-vey! It's your Mo-ther. Ro-bert, you ex-girl friend is on the line. Naturally loud, *Shouters* just don't understand why they are so annoying. One house took up a collection to give their resident shouter elocution lessons.

Wall Watchers stumble into the kitchen each morning, put on the kettle, and stare bleary eyed at a crack in the wall until the water boils. As tempting as it might be, don't try to catch their attention until they're at least halfway through that first cup. Don't bother saying, "Nice crack you're staring at. Changed any since yesterday?" Note: this communication style sometimes occurs in tandem with others.

Morning Chirpers stand in stark contrast to those who need a jolt of caffeine to get going. Chirpers may be the first to fade at a party, but they are up at dawn the next day, puttering in the kitchen, humming an off-key tune, cheery as a bird. *Morning Chirpers* tend to be optimistic people, even in the most bleak situations, which perhaps accounts for the fact that they are occasionally the targets of group house assassination plots. Easily recognizable by their smiles and exceptionally clear eyes, *Chirpers* are also known to sing in the shower and move furniture at 6:00 a.m.

Note Writers are more comfortable with the written than the spoken word. When they have a complaint or want to tell you something, they will scribble it on a scrap and leave it in some conspicuous place: the refrigerator, your bedroom door, your pillow. *Note Writers* come in two types: The *Clever* and the *Obnoxious*. *Clever Note Writers* can be great housemates. One group we interviewed is publishing a year's worth of missives unter the title "Notes from Nona." *Obnoxious Note Writers*, on the other hand, use the medium as a way of taking pot shots at their fellow housemates. Generally these notes are written in an angry hand, with lots of exclamation marks, underlined words, and capital letters. If you notice a tendency towards this sort of notewriting in one of your housemates, nip it in the bud. In most cases, a sharp rap on the knuckles is enough to make your point.

While open communication among housemates is necessary to keep things running smoothly, communication on a more mundane level—passing on phone messages, telling people when rent is due, arranging a party—is equally important. In houses where people share meals, much of this can be taken care of over dinner. But in less structured environments where everyone goes their own way, it can often be frustratingly difficult to get in contact with an errant housemate.

One group house that had twenty-five people living in it over a five-year period worked out a system that included a message board and file with information on how to reach anyone who was not at home. Housemates listed work numbers as well as the numbers of close friends and relatives. When, as often happened, someone moved out, a forwarding address and telephone number were included in the file. Such an arrangement has the additional advantage of making it easy to trace a person trying to skip out on unpaid bills.

Because people spend so much time in the group house kitchen, it is a natural place to leave messages. Often, the refrigerator, an institution in itself, becomes an information kiosk for housemates, with notices, bills, postcards, and cartoons on display. Unfortunately, refrigerators can also be a sort of pillory where housemates are publicly shamed for their misdeeds.

It's temptingly easy to chastise a delinquent housemate by posting a note on a message board or refrigerator. For one thing, you don't have to deal with the person directly, so it can be an ideal way to give vent to unmitigated anger. However, be forewarned: housemates cited nasty notes as one of the most annoying aspects of group living. No matter how you write a note, it is impersonal, and it is bound to generate an angry reaction.

"One morning I found a note on the refrigerator accusing me of eating someone's leftover chicken," recalled Joanne, an advertising copywriter. "That really pissed me off. Especially because I never even touched it."

Jim, in his late twenties, lived in a house with a chronic note writer. One day, as he was about to put some bread in his housemate's toaster oven, he noticed a sign that made his blood boil. "The note said 'Don't abuse me' with a cutesey-pie smiley face. That really bothered me," he said. "You got something to tell me, say it to my face."

House Meetings and the Art of Creative Compromise

Sometimes problems result from the clear-cut abuse of a house law or an individual member's rights. More often, though, they come about because someone has broken an unspoken or private rule.

Although a note written in a fit of pique may be the most convenient way to express these private boundaries, it certainly is not the most constructive. Of course, notes are preferable to swallowing one's feelings and, like the woman in John's house, acting bitter and resentful towards others.

A house meeting is another way to bring these unavoidable conflicts into the open so they can be resolved. Meetings make it easier to deal with house tensions because they provide a structure, a forum for airing complaints, that is removed enough from the battleground for people to be more objective and reasonable. If sparks are set off between housemates, they can be better controlled in a meeting.

Some houses have weekly meetings, other schedule them monthly or semi-monthly. Still others hold them only as needed or when a new housemate joins the group. The frequency is not important. What is important is that meetings are held at all. A house that never has meetings is a house where people can do little more than complain about conditions or pack up their belongings and leave.

"As soon as a problem comes up, it is discussed. Even if it seems like a little thing," said Bill, who lives in a house that holds weekly meetings. When people were too busy to schedule one every week, Bill found tensions were much more evident. "We try to take care of problems before they develop into crises. It's just a matter of talking to each other."

However, you should not think of meetings strictly as a time for dealing with conflicts and preventing them. Meetings also provide a time for hashing through the many technical problems groups encounter in running a house. They give people a chance to make decisions collectively about issues that affect their home.

Is everyone paying bills on time? Is there a problem with the landlord? Is there a need for another refrigerator? What about the broken toilet on the third floor? Did someone leave the door unlocked last night? What can be done to keep utility bills down? Are some housemates being too noisy when others want to sleep? Should the house have a birthday party for Hank?

These are all questions that can be discussed at a house meeting when you are all assembled for the express purpose of dealing with house issues. Meetings also provide a time for housemates, especially those with busy schedules, to touch base with each other. Bill's group has what they call "check-ins" at their house meetings, a time to share personal experiences and ask the group for support.

Houses that have infrequent meetings often post signs to call everyone together and make agendas of items for discussion. However, it's no easy matter to assemble a quorum in a group house in which five or seven people are leading five or seven separate lives. Someone will always be working late, or having dinner with a friend, or taking an evening class, or be out of town. But if you make a commitment to come together, you will be able to find a common meeting time.

Meeting Guidelines

Meetings need a leader, chairman, or facilitator to keep everyone on track. Some groups appoint a permanent leader, others rotate the job, still others seem to have a "natural" leader who takes over. When you are discussing a personal matter, it is wise to pick a member who is not involved in the dispute to mediate.

Group discussions can get bogged down in trivia and can drag on for hours. Decide how much time you are willing to spend on the meeting and stick to it. Limiting a meeting may seem impossible, but with a little discipline, you can take care of everything within the allotted time.

The same issues come up again and again, and you forget the decisions you make in previous meetings. While you don't have to take complete minutes, it is a good idea to jot down a few notes about what you discuss each time.

Reserve some time at the end of the meeting to summarize.

That way, even if you are deadlocked on some issues, you can feel better about the items that were resolved.

Making an Agenda

Just as you need to make records of your meetings, you might also find it helpful to start off with a written list of topics to be discussed. If nothing else, an agenda outlining the major issues will keep things on course (Example 3). Typically, meetings start with house-related matters—finances, maintenance, or miscellaneous problems—before proceeding to the personal issues. Such a strategy gets the easy-to-solve problems out of the way early, leaving the group with the energy and initiative to tackle the more complex personal matters. However, you may want to avoid the personal altogether in your house meetings. As Suzie put it:

I was having trouble with Elaine, it was a problem of our friendship and had nothing to do with the rest of the group. It was up to us to resolve whatever was happening between us in our own way, on our own terms.

Example 3.3: A Sample Agenda for a Full-Scale House Meeting

I. House matters:
- money—how can we cut our utility bills?
- work—the refrigerator needs to be defrosted, the bathrooms are dirty
- emergencies—plumber for broken toilet on third floor
- misc.—birthday party for Hank?

II. Personal problems:
- Judy has complaints about the food group and wants to leave

III. Check-ins

IV. Summary

Often, a practical matter becomes the focus of what is basically a personal issue. In Linda's house, for instance, there was a battle recently over the telephone—a frequent source of friction in group houses. Linda felt that one housemate, a freelance writer, was monopolizing the telephone. She resented the fact that it was virtually impossible to make or receive calls because of the business that was being conducted out of the house. Furthermore, no one made much of an effort to answer the telephone since it was almost always for the same person, and the phone would ring for an unnecessarily long time.

After brooding about the situation for a while, Linda decided to bring it up at a meeting. "It turned out there were a lot of emotional issues underlying it," she said. In this case, the highly charged issue of telephone ethics was further complicated by the fact that Linda and the writer had never taken the time to get properly acquainted. Instead, they nurtured mutual suspicions compounded over time. "I discovered that she had certain misconceptions about me, and I had certain misconceptions about her. Finally we sat down and talked it all out," Linda said.

Linda's housemates also discussed the possibility of putting in another telephone, to be shared by everyone, as well as getting a separate line for the writer's business. In the meantime, the group resolved to make shorter calls, pick up the telephone as soon as it rang, and generally be more considerate of each other. "We usually don't get away from a meeting without saying we are going to do something," Linda commented.

Group Decision Making—Consensus vs. Majority Rule

The way decisions are made in a group house is often as important as the decisions themselves. Through the decision-making process, members control the complicated systems of group life. In some houses, particularly less organized ones, there are no set procedures for making decisions. The senior housemate may, by dint of so many years in the house, have the final and sometimes the only say. Often, the loudest or most forceful member gets his way. Other houses work by precedent, regardless of the wishes of the members. A more egalitarian method is to decide issues by a majority vote or a consensus of the group.

Voting is perhaps the most common way to make a group decision. It is easy, quick, and most people are willing to accede to the group's wishes. If for example, four out of six housemates really do not see the need to get another refrigerator, then obviously, most people don't want that extra refrigerator. Of course, a second refrigerator might be nice, but the two who originally wanted it can probably continue very well without one.

The more serious and delicate the matter, however, the more important it is that everybody be truly satisfied with the decision. Calling for a consensus on an issue will guarantee that everyone has taken part in resolving a particular dilemma and that everyone's voice—however small—is considered in the process. Finally, it assures that all members endorse the group's decision. It may well take longer to reach a consensus, especially in a large group, but the extra effort means the ultimate choice will be a strong one.

Some groups look for consensus on every issue. They simply will not make a decision unless everyone approves. Take, for example, the house that was deadlocked over which brand of toothpaste to buy. One faction endorsed Crest, another wanted Gleem, and a third demanded a natural brand. After two weeks of marathon meetings, lobbying, and even bribery, the group eventually broke down and members bought their own tubes.

If you find the process somewhat unwieldy, you might want to reserve consensus for special situations, such as deciding on a new housemate.

Pam, who lives in a house where everyone must agree before a new member moves in, explained:

Basically it's your space to live in, and if you object to somebody living there—for whatever reasons—there shouldn't have to be a democratic decision on that. It's a gut decision, and if even one person's guts say no, then that prospective housemate should not move in.

Pam said consensus works in her house because people are less likely to make backroom deals and cut capricious decisions on each other. "It pulls people together, rather than pulling them apart."

However, for consensus to work, everyone in your house must feel free to express feelings openly before the group. By the same token, the group must be interested in hearing each member's ideas and must be respectful of them. Finally, individuals must be willing to put the group's well-being ahead of their private considerations.

The Delicate Task of Kicking a Housemate Out

What do you do when you find yourself stuck with someone you absolutely cannot stand? Someone who is irresponsible, argumentative, destructive, or just plain disgusting? Someone who leaves underwear in the bathroom, refuses to even wash dishes, picks his nose over the sugar bowl? No matter how carefully you screen prospective housemates, no matter how patient and forgiving a person you are, you may one day discover you picked a rotten egg. In one house, for example, a man insisted on answering the front door in the nude, offending housemates and guests. In another, an unstable woman tried to commit suicide. In still another, a man had such an abrasive personality that no one would talk to him.

The only solution is to ask the housemate to move out. This happens when a person clearly oversteps the group's boundaries or becomes too self-absorbed to participate in the spirit of the house. Unlike a good melodrama, there is no crook that appears suddenly from the wings to yank the offending member offstage. You will have to get rid of this person yourself, look her square in the eye and ask her to leave. Admittedly, this is an ugly, unpleasant job, but you *can* do it with delicacy.

By handling the matter in a positive, rather than negative way, you can make the experience easier on everyone. Point out the much happier and calmer existence that will result. Present the decision as a group decision, not as the whim of one particular member, if indeed this is the case. Make an effort to help the offending member find new housing, and be flexible in the face of problems the person might have finding a new place to live. If you know someone is on the way out, you may find yourself acting more generously.

Of course, there are times when a gross violation of house ethics calls for rash action. This is particularly true when you are dealing with money-related matters. Although some people are willing to help a housemate out in an economic pinch, no one wants to do it regularly. In fact, financial negligence can generate so much anger that house mates feel justified in resorting to draconian measures to make their point.

Peter, an electronics engineer, told the story of the very spoiled woman in his group house who racked up a $200 telephone bill and simply refused to pay it. After trying everything, from gentle peer pressure to threats of bodily harm, and dismissing the possibility of sending her a singing telegram because it was too expensive, the group settled on a radical solution: One weekend, when the woman was out of town, they changed the locks on the doors and sold her possessions in a rummage sale. Although they didn't make enough money to cover the unpaid bill, the housemates were pleased that they had once and for all purged themselves of a serious financial problem. "It was very satisfying," Peter recalled.

Money Madness

Why is money so often the cause of conflict in group houses? Sociologists will tell you it is because money is bound up with fundamental human emotions, such as possessiveness and self-image. On a more basic level, the importance of money is obvious—it is the main management issue facing any group, essential to the house's existence from day to day, month to month.

Because of its importance, people often act "funny," if not downright strange, about money. Even married couples can come to blows when one person's ideas about how financial resources should be used clash with another's. It may sound like a truism, but it bears repeating: A solid financial arrangement among housemates contributes immeasurably to the stability and well-being of the group. This is particularly true in houses where people live together for strictly financial reasons. But whatever the situation, money is always the bottom line in any group house.

Keep in mind that running a house is in many ways like running a business. If you were involved in a business, you would agree with your partners to take on certain financial responsibilities. You would collect money from each other, pay it out, and generally live up to your commitments, or the enterprise would fail. Furthermore, you would decide amongst yourselves the mechanics of the business that would ensure your economic survival.

Financial arrangements vary widely from house to house, ranging from situations in which members pool all or part of their incomes to those in which people share only expenses. Most group houses, however, are structured so that each member will gain the maximum economic benefit from the group with the minimum individual contribution.

Divvying Up Financial Responsibility

Jesse, an artist who lives in a loosely structured house in Chapel Hill, North Carolina, with two of his closest friends, said,

We never kept accounts. There were times when I had very little money coming in, and Nina and Jack paid for everything. And there were times when my income was stable enough that I could buy food for everyone, or pay the entire phone bill, or take care of a whole month's rent. The finances worked well, and we never questioned the appropriateness of it.

Needless to say, Jesse's arrangement is an unusual one. More commonly, the group makes a formal plan for divvying up financial responsibility. Often one person takes the job of house accountant permanently, especially if that person is adept at handling money or owns a calculator. "I'm terrible at doing books, but Charles, who was an accountant by training, took care of the finances," explained Gene, who rented a house in Austin, Texas, for five years. "Connie had a very effective way of asking people for money," he continued. "She didn't nag, and she didn't come down too hard, so she was in charge of collections."

Another group "hired" one of their less solvent members to be house manager by knocking $20 off the rent each month in return for service. The manager's responsibilities included keeping the bathrooms stocked with toilet paper and soap, paying bills, collecting money from members, and dealing with repairmen and the landlord.

You may want to rotate the job of overseeing finances among group members, as you would any chore, or you can let each person take care of a specific bill. Groups that are just starting out, especially student groups, may find the latter arrangement a good way to resolve the problem of whose name goes on the bill. After all, if your name is on the oil, electricity, or telephone bill, you are financially on the hook, but there are advantages to having a bill in your name. You can, for example, use a utility bill to prove residence or show that you are a stable, credit-worthy member of the community.

If you are planning to leave your house, switch the accounts over to a current member's name. The move may cost a bit more money in the short run but could avert financial and legal problems later. Students who live in group houses that they plan to vacate in the summer and return to in the fall face a special problem. On one hand, you don't want to be stuck with a subletee's bills. On the other hand, you don't want to have to pay to have the services reconnected under your name a few months later. A good solution is to keep things as they are, but make the subletee sign an agreement guaranteeing to pay all bills between June and August. Or you can pay the bills yourself and adjust the rent to reflect the cost. Steve and Chris, students at the University of North Carolina at Chapel Hill, came to fisticuffs recently over this very matter. Steve, who was staying in the house over the summer, wanted to keep the electricity bill in Chris's name, thereby saving a $75 deposit. But Chris didn't trust Steve to pay the bill and insisted on turning the electricity off. Before long, the entire house was involved in the brawl. In the end, Chris, who had the account with the utility company, got his way.

On the Subject of Subletting

Group dwellers tend to be more than a little uneasy about subletting their rooms. There's the obvious anxiety over admitting an unknown quantity into your house while your names are on the lease thereby making you liable for any damages. There's the cloud of financial worry hanging over each sublettor's head. You wonder whether you'll lose money during your absence, and of course, everybody wants to come out even. Chances are nobody will come out even unless everybody in the house works out the details together, well in advance of the departure date.

Student sublettors, in their eagerness to skip town after exams, often fail to confer with housemates about their expectations. For instance, Maria, a University of Chicago student in a hurry to leave her house after graduation, didn't try to find a subletee for her room. Yet, she became irate when she heard from another housemate, Charlotte, that someone had stayed in her room during the month of July without paying. Maria then wrote a nasty letter to Charlotte demanding reimbursement. It put Charlotte in a bind since the unofficial subletee was her best friend. Rather than ask her friend to pay up, Charlotte sent Maria money from her own pocket. It was a gesture designed to keep alive the tenuous but congenial relationship they had developed as housemates. Unfortunately, their relationship was fractured beyond repair after that summer because of the mutual resentments they harbored. To avoid situations like this, meet with housemates to find out where your household stands on the following questions:

- Is each person responsible for finding his own subletee and deciding on the rent?
- Will the rent charged be a fraction of the rent for a specific room, or will rents of all vacant rooms be combined and equal fractions charged to subletees?
- Who should interview subletees—the sublettor, the remaining housemates, or both?
- Will the subletee be required to sign a contract with the sublettor? With the landlord?
- Will housemates' friends be expected to pay for extended stays in the event that a subletee can't be found?

Remember, if you do entrust the finding of a subletee to your housemates, then take what you get and don't quibble for a few more dollars. A lot of negotiation goes on between those vying for vacancies and those parcelling them out, and you'll be lucky to get more than half your rent back.

Checking Out Checking Accounts

One way to get money out of your housemates to cover shared obligations is to ask them to dig into their pockets each time an expense comes up. An easier method is to set up a house checking account at a local bank. Then housemates can make deposits into the account, and a single check can be written for each of the group's expenses, as Ralph explained.

> *Right from the start we prevailed upon a major bank in San Francisco to set up a joint signature account. Anyone who moved in was asked to join the account. A joint signing meant that any person had access to the group's money, since the bank card had all our signatures on it. It meant that anyone could conceivably steal the whole account, so there was a basic element of trust involved. When we were considering a new housemate, we'd have to ask ourselves, "Would I trust this person with my money?" The account became the final test for new housemates.*

With all the possibilities for free checking and even interest bearing accounts, it's a good idea to shop around before you commit the group's money to any bank. Because groups often deal with large sums of money, collecting and paying out as much as $1,500 a month, interest bearing checking accounts could prove a boon. Also, many banks offer premiums. One house managed to stock its kitchen with a blender, a toaster oven, a popcorn popper, and a juicer by opening accounts at various banks around town. Another house got luggage for every member, and whenever someone would join the group, the housemates made a point of scaring up another premium as a welcoming gesture.

Group House Bookkeeping 101

Most groups handle expenses in one of two ways:

• *Monthly Reckoning*
Housemates pay separately for whatever expenses come their way, including large bills and incidental expenses, and keep a log of the transactions. At the end of each month, the group sits down for a marathon reckoning session. Any excess (deficit) is added to (subtracted from) each housemate's basic rent.

• *Budgeted Reckoning*
Housemates pay, more or less, a fixed monthly sum (an average operating cost) into the group account, and all major purchases are made from it. Usually there is a "kitty" with up to $100 a month for smaller purchases or emergencies.

The *Monthly Reckoning* method is more flexible because it allows housemates who are short of cash early in the month to slide while the others carry them. You might also find it convenient if you are prone to make spur-of-the-moment purchases and if you basically trust your housemates. However, reckoning day can be chaotic to say the least. Simon, a researcher at the Environmental Protection Agency who lives in a loosely structured group house, described his financial system as ". . . a terribly complicated mess that's caused all kinds of problems."

The *Budgeted Reckoning* system, while more structured, avoids that end-of-the-month scramble to straighten out finances.

People are less likely to haggle over expenses if they pay in one lump sum. Furthermore, short-term residents end up paying a more equitable share of household expenses because they pay an average figure. That way, bills that come only twice a year or quarterly are added into the economic equation.

If you do have a kitty, make sure someone is responsible for overseeing where the money goes. While housemates don't always steal from the petty cash fund, a guest might be tempted to take a dollar or two. Also, housemates have been known to "borrow" five bucks from the stash, and then forget to pay it back. So if you want the money to be there when you need it, have someone take care of it.

When, at long last, you've decided how to apportion finances, you may want to adopt some kind of bookkeeping system to keep track of your expenses on a regular basis. Here, then, is how you can easily record your house financial transactions. See Example 3.4 for the Monthly Reckoning System and Example 3.5 for the Budgeted Reckoning System.

Major Expenses For Group Houses

Rent, usually is the group's greatest expense each month. In some houses, rent is related to room size with the person living in the master bedroom paying as much as $50 more than whoever lives in the converted closet. On the other hand, there is an egalitarian aspect to dividing the rent evenly, despite room size, that some groups find attractive.

"People get to move into the better rooms by seniority and I like that," said Rebecca, who waited a year to get the large, sunny bedroom she now occupies. "It means that even though I make one of the lowest salaries in the group, I can live in one of the nicest rooms in the house."

EXAMPLE 3.4 -- "Monthly Reckoning" system of bookkeeping

1982 November		Paul	Carol	Martin	Nancy		
11 2	Groceries	54.80					
11 4	Lightbulbs			2.98		①	
11 7	Electricity bill			34.21			
11 9	Groceries				51.18		
11 11	Party expenses	20.00	40.00	20.00			
11 13	Phone bill			30.00	30.00		
11 16	Groceries		59.82				
11 19	Toaster Oven				48.99		
11 23	Groceries			57.12			
11 25	Firewood		80.00				
11 28	Newspaper			10.00			
11 30	Groceries	54.82				③	
	② TOTAL EXPENSES	129.62	179.82	154.31	130.17	= $593.92	
		- 148.48	-148.48	-148.48	-148.48	÷ 4......$148.48 ④	
		-18.86	31.34	5.83	-18.31	⑤	
	Rent	187.50	187.50	187.50	187.50	⑥	
		+ 18.86	-31.34	- 5.83	+18.31		
11 30	Rent checks	206.36	156.16	181.67	205.81	= $750.00	

① Enter description of expense and amount under purchaser's name.

② Total individual purchases.

③ Add individual totals to make the house total.

④ Divide total expenses by number of housemates. This yields each member's share of the total expenses. As you can see, some members paid more or less than their share.

⑤ Compute the difference between each individual total and each person's share of total house expenses.

⑥ Those who underpaid on expenses pay a rent surcharge for the month; those who overpaid are given a rent discount.

⑦ Each rent payment plus individual purchases should be the same -- in this case $335.98. For instance, Paul's purchases (129.62) + his rent (206.36) = 335.98.

Example 3.5 -- "Budgeted Reckoning" Bookkeeping System

82			Credits	Debits	Balance
11	1	Paul's check	375.00		375.00
11	1	Carol's check	375.00		750.00
11	1	Martin's check	375.00		1125.00
11	1	Nancy's check	375.00		1500.00
11	1	Rent - check #358		750.00	750.00
11	2	Groceries - check #359		54.80	695.20
11	4	Lightbulbs - check #360		2.98	692.22
11	7	Electric bill - check #361		34.21	658.01
11	9	Groceries - check #362		51.18	606.83
11	11	Party expenses - check #363		80.00	526.83
11	13	Phone bill - check #364		60.00	466.83
11	16	Groceries - check #365		60.27	406.56
11	19	Toaster Oven - check #366		48.99	357.57
11	23	Groceries - check #367		57.12	300.45
11	25	Firewood - check #368		80.00	220.45
11	28	Newspaper - check #369		10.00	210.45
11	30	Groceries - check #370		54.82	155.63
11	30	Paul's check	375.00		491.73
11	30	Carol's check	375.00		857.82
11	30	Martin's check	375.00		1193.91
11	30	Nancy's check	375.00		1500.00

(1) Each person pays enough to bring total in house account up to $1,500.00.

(2) The house treasurer writes direct checks for all household expenses. (If account is joint signing account, then any house member can write checks.)

Whatever system you choose, be consistent. Suddenly deciding to charge more for the master bedroom with the marble fireplace is not only unfair, it can have a disastrous effect on housemates. Dan, who waited patiently for an opportunity to get a bigger room, actually left his house when he realized he would have to pay extra:

Since I paid equal rent when I lived in the small room,
I assumed I'd continue paying the same amount when
I moved into the better room. But Frank wanted to
charge a higher price because we were going through
a rough financial time. I got so fed up with the whole
thing I moved out.

Utilities. Includes oil, gas, and electricity and, in some cities, water and trash removal. Utility bills, especially for heating, can run quite high in the older houses many groups rent. Often there are no storm windows, no insulation, and no incentives for landlords to make such houses energy efficient. Because utility costs can vary so widely from month to month, season to season, your house may want to average a year's expenses and pay a constant sum each month. Check with your utility company. They may have a strategy to help you level your utility costs throughout the year.

Averaging is also helpful in the situation of short-term housemates who move out before a semi-annual water bill comes. To average, you will need to keep records so you know how much it costs to maintain the house over a year. If you are just starting out, ask your landlord or the former occupants about utility costs.

Food. Is sometimes kept separate from the other expenses. For more information on the economics of group house food systems, see Chapter 4.

Telephone. Is quite inexpenxive when shared by a group. Most houses have more than one telephone. Some may have more than one telephone number. Usually, you divide the basic service charge and everyone pays their own long-distance calls, adding tax. If your group makes a lot of long-distance calls, usually more than $100 a month, an MCI or SPRINT Service is worth considering.

Post the telephone bill in a prominent place each month and have people initial calls, a process that can take as long as two weeks. Inevitably, there are mystery numbers, calls people forgot they made, calls a guest made. Occasionally, calls that no one made will show up on the bill. "You always have to be prepared to spend a few extra dollars for unclaimed calls, but it's worth it—you get it back *spiritually*," said John, who lived in a group house with a joint checking account.

Taxes, Home Improvement Loans. Are considerations only for group home owners. See Chapter 6 for more information.

Maid Service. Is an obvious luxury that could well be the answer to those chores that are never done. One house eliminated all cleaning responsibilities, except dishes and bedrooms, by hiring a so-called "household technician." Other groups simply have a maid come in once or twice a month. The weekly $45 fee, divided among the six people in the house, seemed a small price to pay for domestic harmony.

Household Items. Includes soap, toilet paper, detergent, cleaning goods, kitchen utensils, tools, newspaper or magazine subscriptions, cable television, and even pet care expenses. While this category may account for only a few dollars at a time, smaller household expenses do add up. If you share the cost equally, you will be more likely to replace that roll of toilet paper when it's gone.

Miscellaneous. Don't overlook occasional expenses. You may find a terrific deal on chairs or lamps at a neighbor's yard sale. Or you may have to replace a broken window or call a locksmith in the eleventh hour.

Paul, who lives in a house where everyone earns a modest income, learned that one painless way to make a large group purchase is to collect a few dollars from each housemate along with the rent. Then squirrel this money away until the required sum is reached. On this installment plan, Paul's house purchased a washing machine and a clothes dryer. Paul explains:

We try to keep a surplus in the account, and often we are a month ahead. This means that when we need a new roommate we aren't forced into taking the first person that comes along, just because we need the money. It also means we don't have to collar people for rent or go through an "end-of-the-month" economic crunch. Our principle is pay first and argue later.

Sometimes I wonder why I'm paying more rent than I absolutely have to, but it is awfully nice to be able to have someone shovel your walk when it snows and not have to collect pennies from everyone.

Ironing Out the Kinks

Unfortunately, group house finances are never as simple as identifying expenses, collecting money, and paying the bills. There are always a few kinks in every system, kinks that must be resolved. As your house grows and its financial systems evolve, you will have to work out solutions to the unique economic situation your group poses.

What do you do, for example, when a member is away from the house for a long period of time? Do you have a commitment to pay for all household expenses, regardless of whether you are around to enjoy them? Should someone on vacation or on a business trip have to contribute to utility bills? When Charlie, a paralegal in a Washington, D.C., law firm, developed a heart condition that landed him in the hospital for three months, he arranged to pay the rent on his room but not the utilities.

And what about housemates who spend most of their time at a lover or friend's house? Are these people full or partial housemates? Some groups, particularly those that buy food and eat together, have devised elaborate systems for determining how much money a person owes. Under such a system, a member who is away for a certain period of time (four days of the week or two weeks of the month) would pay a full share. But if the member is absent for three weeks he would get reimbursed.

There is the problem of guests and how to account for them financially. You may feel that hospitality is an important part of a shared living situation and ask your guests for no remuneration. On the other hand, you might like the idea of guests pulling their own financial weight. Or you might want to ask your guest to contribute to food or participate in household chores.

What are the economics of being a couple? If two people share one room, do they pay as individuals or should they split the rent? And what about utilities? One possibility is to let the couple divide the cost of the room and pay for utilities separately. Another option would be for the couple to pay for a share and a half of total house expenses. Keep in mind, though, that extra bodies mean more hands to help with housework.

Of all financial problems that can plague groups, the most serious is irresponsibility. How do you deal with someone who will not pay bills? Most group house dwellers take a dim view of housemates who constantly break financial agreements. Because late payments often result in fines, or extra deposits for the group, some houses have rules stipulating that the person who causes a late fee has to pay it. Occasionally the house shoulders the loss, but most people are reluctant to pay any more than is absolutely necessary to keep the house going.

The final solution, of course, is to ask a person to leave the group. But after the offending member is gone, what can you do about that pile of unpaid bills? One option is for the house to absorb the loss, although this is perhaps the least satisfactory solution. You can also try harassing the ex-housemate into submission, but chances are you won't get very far. A third possiblity is to try squeezing some money from the housemate's family. No one interviewed mentioned collection agencies, but don't rule them out as a last resort. The only real leverage you have against a financially delinquent housemate is the security deposit.

Security Deposits

Security deposits serve the same purpose among housemates that they do between realtor and rentor: they ensure that occupants do not damage the house, shirk financial responsibilities, or leave without giving adequate notice. With a month's rent on the line, you are likely to think twice before disappearing.

In houses with high turnover, the incoming member pays a deposit to the outgoing member so that everyone eventually gets his money back. Carrying this concept even further, one house asks for a room deposit of $50 from new housemates as soon as they are accepted. It is deducted from the new member's share of the security deposit. It is not returned if someone promises to move in and then changes his mind at the last minute. This way the group does not get stuck. And Don's household goes *one more* smart step beyond:

Everybody that originally moved in had to pay a security deposit, but we decided, since nobody made a lot of money, that they wouldn't have to pay us the whole $290 dollars (rent and deposit) right away. They pay $50 and then pay the bills of the person that moved out (who didn't get a deposit back) until it equals $145. Or they refund the difference between what they paid on bills to the person who moved out.

A last word of advice: When a house is disbanding, the group is entitled to the original deposit, plus yearly interest on the sum. But you usually won't get it unless you ask for it. Check your local laws.

Advanced Group Living: Scene 2. From the Sweat of their Brows: Dudley House, Inc.

Just up the street from the Rhode Island Hospital in Providence, in a modest neighborhood of sturdy but neglected Victorian houses and lots ajumble with weeds, stands Dudley House, Inc.—a monument to group living squeezed from the very sweat of those who share the space.

Downstairs, Debbie insulates a window well from the winter winds while nearby Newell hooks up the back doorbell. Upstairs, Jeff sands and scrapes the molding in his bedroom. Doug, who has just installed a sink in the second floor bathroom, is on the telephone, negotiating for a new toilet. A vat of tomato sauce, tended by Diana, simmers on the stove. In the garden outside, Keith tucks a row of young tomato plants into a bed of freshly raked soil.

When they bought the house for $1,000 last year, Debbie, Jeff and Doug knew they were getting a "handyman special." Abandoned for many months, two fires had ravaged the place, and the local urchins had smashed all seventy-two windows. It took several days just to cart away the accumulated debris.

But the group managed to do their work with a momentum that has carried them over the rough spots: lack of help, lack of funds, and, occasionally, lack of enthusiasm. "We really had no idea this project would be such an enormous undertaking," said Debbie, as she stapled a sheet of fiberglass in place.

Aside from taking on the task of renovating the twenty-four-room structure, the threesome formed Dudley House, Inc., a non-profit organization that administers a local land trust. Each summer a patchwork of community gardens sprout on the empty property the trust has acquired.

Though unfinished, Dudley House is an expression of the hard-earned sense of self-sufficiency these people prize so highly. But even more than the immediate satisfaction of being able to live by their efforts, the group wants the house to serve as an example to a community that is mired in its inability to improve. "I didn't want to just restore a house," said Debbie. "I wanted to learn about survival at its most basic level and then demonstrate this knowledge to the local community."

A small but dynamic woman, Debbie got involved in the project after graduating from Brown University with a degree in literature. Jeff, a geology major who had construction experience, said he was attracted to the house because he was "between things" and liked the idea of working to improve a poor neighborhood without spoiling it. They teamed up with Doug, a computer engineer in a Providence-based solar technology firm. As the most solvent member of the group, Doug had a strong enough income to sign the $19,000 home improvement mortgage. "Between us we had the skills to make it work," said Jeff. "We formed in effect the heart, hands, and head of the project."

The other people who have gravitated to Dudley House, Diana, Newell, Bundy, Nancy, Jim and the many friends who visit for an afternoon or a week, contribute what they can: money or work, usually both. If a motto were inscribed on the threshold of the house it would have to be: Pitch In. Everyone pitches in, and in so doing, leaves his mark on the house—a wall here, a window or a fixture there. And everyone takes something as well—a new skill, a feeling of accomplishment, a sense of effort shared.

By flexing their collective muscle, the group has installed the wiring and plumbing, rebuilt the chimney and all the walls, and set up woodburning stoves. They cultivate an urban garden so productive it feeds them through the winter, tend three hives of purposefully buzzing bees, and have crafted a whirring rooftop windmill that generates enough energy to light the downstairs hall. Still, much work remains to be done. "With such an overwhelming project," said Debbie, "you have to focus on the small tasks, take solace in the small victories." When tallied though, these victories seem substantial enough.

However steeped in the ideology of collective activity, Dudley House would not be possible without a firm financial foundation. The project has consumed about $40,000 so far, money these resourceful people have raised in a variety of ways. The core group, which is responsible for gathering and dispensing money, scraped together $1,000 to buy the house from SWAP (Stop Wasting Abandoned Property), a local program dedicated to saving abandoned inner city houses. The city of Providence gave them a $4,500 urban homesteading grant, and through a federal weatherization program they got free insulation worth about $1,500. Then there is the $19,000 mortgage. The group built a greenhouse, a solid post-and-beam structure that warms the house while it coddles their seedlings, with a $6,500 competitive Department of Energy grant. They raised an additional $5,000 from local residents for their land trust. Another $3,000 came from savings and contributions by family and friends.

To make sure all these dollars make sense, there are three checking accounts—one for Dudley House, Inc., one for the household, and one for the community land trust and garden project.

It hasn't been easy coordinating the efforts of the group's eight very independent members, but somehow the work gets done. Owners Debbie, Doug, and Jeff, form a sort of "security council" on house matters and meet Fridays in a local bar to plan the next week's work and hash out major problems. In addition, they come together early in the morning on each work day.

"We've had to create our systems and procedures as we go, which is both exciting and difficult," explained Debbie. After trying several unsatisfactory set-ups, the owners now work on their house four days a week, an arrangement that covers their rent. The others pay $150 a month rent, with no obligation to work. But everyday spent painting and scraping knocks $10 off the rent. This money is then plowed back into the house, paying off the mortgage and buying supplies. When it comes time to leave, the owners figure they will have about $10,000 in sweat equity in the house.

Beyond this complicated and rather arbitrary financial arrangement, a system Debbie calls "funny money," are the baseline economic considerations necessary to maintain any group house: food, utilities, supplies, and furniture. While the garden and wood-burning stove cut the major costs considerably, housemates kick in an extra $30 a month that includes $15 for food (bought in bulk), a $10 energy fee to spread the cost of the winter through all seasons and housemates, and $5 for larger household purchases.

The chores, such as shopping and cleaning, emptying the trash and compost, gardening, and even baking bread rotate among the members each week. "In the beginning we had some pretty bad bread," said Jeff as he pulled four loaves of fresh onion bread from the oven, "but now just about everyone can bake a decent loaf."

In the evening, people gather around the table for a meal of lasagna, salad from the garden, and homemade onion-garlic bread. It has been a long day, filled with hammering and scraping, carting and weeding. Tomorrow will be equally long. But little by little the work is done. Despite the seemingly endless effort the project requires, Dudley House is a place where pride is plentiful and hopes are high.

"Of course, we look forward to the time when all the work will be finished," said Doug. "But we also know that the process is as important as the product. Sometimes it's easy to forget, but that's why we're here."

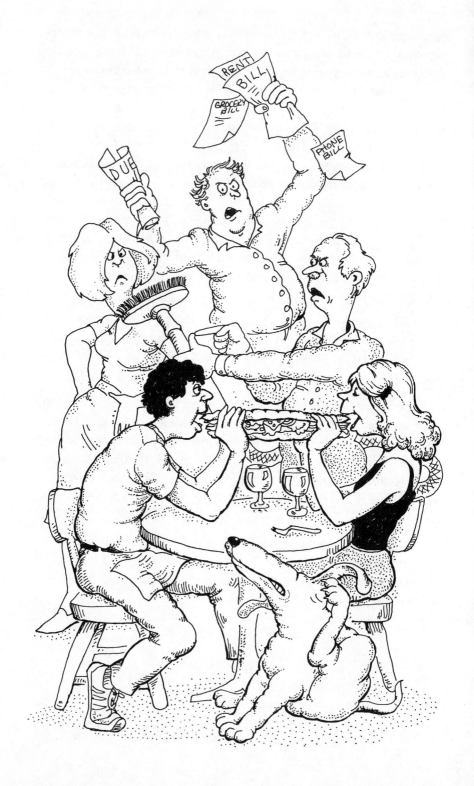

Group House Nitty Gritty I: Eating and Cleaning

Group House Domestic Stew   Not long after you've moved into a group house (and perhaps even before your first house meeting), you will have a taste of that unique concoction, "Group House Domestic Stew." To make, a household need only . . .

Take three or more (try to stop at ten) assorted individuals of any age, shape, size or color.

Add one refrigerator with last month's food bill taped onto it *or* substitute seven cartons of milk and a variety of mysterious foil packets and plastic containers with cryptic labels on them.

Mix together with: a mop, rags, Ajax, a gallon of ammonia, and a workwheel created after months of discussion.

Toss in the following:

> a dash of sexual tension

> a few housemates who have overstayed their welcome

> a dog (or cat) that needs a good dose of flea powder

> one television set and three stereos

> a Salvation Army couch, some cinder blocks and planks, and a toaster oven.

Mix well in one house or apartment to make a steamy brew of individuals with their housekeeping standards, habits, and practices struggling to live under one roof without boiling over.

The problems that surface in group houses and threaten to blow the roof off usually center around one or more of the following issues: food and how it's procured, paid for, stored, and eaten; housework; sexual tension among housemates not to mention their "lovers and other strangers"; sharing space and possessions; and pets. Some scholars of group living theorize that these concerns, especially food, money, and housecleaning, are so emotionally laden because they correspond to Freud's developmental stages of "food (oral gratification, nurturing), money (anal retentiveness, possessiveness), and work (phallic mastery, competence)."[3]

Don't take a crash course in Freudian psychology before you attempt group living, but it does help to recognize when domestic squabbles mask disharmony more complex than a simple conflict between "clean" and "messy." If you find yourself in a heated fracas with a housemate over something that would ordinarily be considered trivial—a few crumbs on the table or a past due bill of 89¢—stop trying to disentangle the branches of the problem, and look instead at its roots.

Often the roots of group house domestic troubles will go back to how each housemate was brought up. Not only will you have individual housemates to contend with but their family backgrounds and myths as well. The spirit of Ann's mother hovers over the range saying, "Pour the bacon grease in a jar and save it." Your ex-wife butts in, "No, dear, put it in a can and leave it outside for the birds." Tad's father says, "Hey, what the hell, I always told you to pour it right down the sink." When the sink starts burping and Tad runs to call the plumber, you may just have to grin and bear it.

The ability to tolerate everyone's differences regarding the nitty gritty issues (major or minor) of daily life while you learn to compromise will go far to help even the most diverse group function harmoniously. However, if tolerance and compromise were all you needed to turn would-be bones of contention into bones of contentment, there would be no use for this chapter or the next, let alone this whole handbook. In this chapter and the next there is advice, helpful attitudes, and tips to keep your group house domestic stew simmering merrily away.

The Group House Food Spectrum

Of all the issues mentioned, food is probably the biggest boon or bane of a group house's existence. It can draw your house together around the kitchen table or keep housemates as separate as snap-locked Tupperware containers. When people talk about whether they share food with their housemates, a kind of continuum of group house food plans emerges. At one end there are households that buy food and eat it together on a regular basis with housemates taking turns in the kitchen. Next, there are those who purchase collectively yet only eat together once in a blue moon. Then there are households that split costs on only a few staples like flour, eggs, milk, and toothpaste. At the other end of the continuum are housemates who don't share anything but refrigerator and shelf space. People who are at either end seem to be the most staunch defenders of their house's way of handling the food issue.

Joe, twenty-eight, member of a communal fare house said adamantly, "I've always refused to deal with people who wanted to have separate food and cooking. . . . If you're going to live together there's got to be some form of interaction, and if everybody goes their own way so much that they're not even willing to buy food together, then I'm not interested."

Just as adamant is Lise, twenty-three, a flight attendant who lived with three other flight attendants. Each of them had their own refrigerator shelf. Said Lise, "We didn't share food *at all.* Everybody had totally different schedules, totally different eating habits. We kept everything separate. . . . It's the best way to do it."

Generally, houses like Joe's are more cohesive than houses like Lise's. But, that is as far as you can go in generalizing about people and their food arrangments. Forget the myth that all food sharers also share the same political views, eat vegetarian, and practice transcendental meditation. Equally misleading is the assumption that all groups on a laissez-*fare* system like Lise's household are "rich kids, smokers, meat eaters, and bums"—to quote one narrow-minded food sharer. Each group has its own particular reasons for forming its food plan. Your household's task will be to find an arrangement that satisfies everyone.

Enjoying the Communal Fare

Even though housemates who eat communally tend to form a more cohesive household, this aspect of sharing doesn't have to take away from the individuality or autonomy of house members. In houses where individuality runs rampant, the kitchen table can become the intersection point for lives that otherwise never converge, except when housemates stumble out of the bathroom in the morning. On the other hand, housemates who all belong to the same political cause or religious group may join hands around the table in silent prayer before dinner, creating in the circle another symbol of their shared lifestyle.

When you and your housemates come together regularly for generous helpings of tetrazzini, laughter, and conversation, the heated confrontations that can occur during house meetings may be totally eliminated. Lloyd, who had a communal fare arrangement with five other men during their second year of college, expressed a sentiment common among food-sharing groups. "At dinnertime we'd always be gathered as a group and a lot of things that could have been problems or behind-the-back comments came out in jest."

Speaking of students, cooking and eating communally is the perfect initiation to the mysterious world of colanders, slotted spoons, and spaghetti cooked "al dente" instead of "al Mommy." Chances are that most of your housemates will also feel "lost in the kitchen," and it's a conducive atmosphere for creating your first concoction without "pressure to perform." Lastly, food sharing will save you time, provided your household plans meals, shops, and cooks efficiently. If Monday through Friday you are guaranteed a hearty meal at about 7:00, you'll probably consume more food in less time than you would in a dutch treat arrangement. Whatever your good intentions are, you and your housemates should sit down and answer some questions individually before you decide to eat together:

- Do you find cooking an unbearable chore? Would you much prefer to whip up something quick or go out to eat?

- Are you a very picky eater or on a special diet? Do you have very expensive, or at the other extreme, very low-cost tastes?

- Do you hate feeling bound to a schedule, preferring spontaneous get-togethers?

- Do you work late often or find yourself frequently committed during dinner hours?

- Do you feel hesitant about splitting the food bill with housemates?

If you or your housemates answered, yes, to any of these questions, you would be better off finding a more suitable arrangement on the group house food spectrum.

When Soup's On And When it's Off

In deciding which nights will be communal fare nights, take into consideration the number of people you have. If you have four people in your house, you could eat together four nights a week—say from Monday through Thursday. This is a very convenient arrangement for business people or ski bums because it leaves weekends totally free for trips. If you have five people, try five nights a week or four nights with one person "off." We don't have to spell out all the combinations or possibilities for you. Just imagine, if you live with seven others you may only have to cook once every two weeks.

Aside from houses in which one member is a bustling Julia Child who is quite content to cook for others every night, we've found that group dwellers apportion K.P. duty in two ways. Members may volunteer to cook and/or clean dishes on an impromptu basis. "Hey," one person might say, "I'd like to cook lasagna on Monday night." "Great!" another replies, "I'll clean that night and cook the chicken dish I've been meaning to try on Wednesday." After which, everybody bargains for the cooking/cleaning slot. These ad hoc households are, more often than not, composed of people who are so attuned to each other's schedules and preferences that they feel silly sitting down and mapping out domestic routines. In houses with people who are just beginning to know each other, however, developing a cooking schedule is important for forming a house foundation on which relationships can be built. In this situation, it's best to put a sheet up on the refrigerator listing the days of the week and allow everyone to decide which night will be their cooking night (and perhaps what they plan to cook to avoid duplication). But be ready to juggle nights when someone starts a class or has another commitment.

Decide at the outset how you'll clean up after meals. Either the cook cleans up the mess, one other person signs up to clean, or everyone cleans up after the cook. One member of a household that rotated cooking and cleaning nights told how resentment built up when one man felt it was unfair that he had to clean up after a messy cook when he took pains to be neat in preparing dinners. Because of the potential friction and because nothing is so dismal as facing alone the remains of mulligatawny stew for eight, most houses favor cleaning collectively. While everyone bustles around the kitchen, the cook is free to retire to her room, close the door and "sink into the carpet." If your kitchen is too small to accomodate many hands, feet, elbows, sponges, and dishtowels, you could do what a socialist-minded house did—they assigned a primary cleaner and a secondary cleaner.

Don't Do Unto Your Housemate as You Would to Your Mother

You are cooking lasagna for five, and you are proud of yourself as you watch it bubbling merrily in the oven. Three of your housemates come out of their respective rooms and follow the glorious scent to the kitchen. You feel pleased that you coordinated the green beans almondine with the lasagna and garlic bread. You take off your apron thinking that cooking for five people isn't nearly the ordeal you expected when, suddenly, the fifth housemate bursts through the front door. You smile at him, then you notice three other people standing hesitantly in the doorway—three more people looking hungrily at the table. Your elation goes flat as you dish out tiny servings to eight people apologizing to them as if you should have *known* you were serving three extra people...but fuming inside. This could happen to you or one of your housemates if you neglect some simple rules of dining room protocol for the group house:

- Let the cook know at least a day in advance if you are bringing a guest. Similarly, let the cook know in advance if you won't be at dinner.

- Be at dinner on time. Again, if you're going to be late let the cook know in advance. That way you'll be assured of getting some leftovers, and you won't delay dinner for everyone else. If you didn't let the cook know of your tardiness, don't come waltzing in late and expect to see a little hermetically sealed pouch of delicious looking food at your plate.

- Be *nice* to the cook. Maybe it was okay with Mom to toss the food around on your plate, give it a peremptory sniff, and say in your best thirteen-year-old voice, "What *is* this?" Keep telling yourself, "My housemate is not my mother."

With an adventurous attitude and a bold palate you can learn more from shared meals than in a course at the New York School for the Culinary Arts. A word of caution: Don't be a closet veggie and scream at the sight of meat during that first meal together. When you gather to make a cooking schedule, use that time to discuss dietary restrictions. If there are both veggies and carnivores in your house, and you still want to make a go of the shared meal plan, more power to you. You'll probably learn more about tolerance and compromise and experimentation right there at the

dinner table than anywhere else in group house life. If you're adamant about your preferences, shared eating is not for you unless
you find others who share that preference. Believe it or not, there
are even kosher vegetarian households. Just don't try to convert the
average group house with its assortment of mismatched plates to
your way of thinking.

Splitting the Food Bill

Pleasant table manners, good cooking, and cheerful cleaning
make any meal more enjoyable. But the main criterion for a successful food-sharing plan is *how the grocery bills are divided.* When
members of a household can relax and pat their bellies after dinner,
weaving their own tales into the colored fabric of conversation, it's
because they have a system for buying and paying for food that
works. They are also likely to have common attitudes about the
house "consumption process."

In a group house, there are as many ways to pay for food as to
prepare it. Every house inevitably develops its own style and its
own quirks. When people are just starting out, they usually rotate
shopping. The shopper writes a personal check for the groceries,
posts the receipt, and everyone settles up later or, preferably,
sooner. After a while, most households can tell how much they
spend on groceries each week. To eliminate the lag time between
when the shopper pays and when the housemates fork over their
cash, it's a good idea to pay in advance. If you have a house account
you can have everyone advance $25.00 or so a week. The shopper
writes the check from that reserve. For reasons outlined in Chapter
3, don't deposit food money into a kitty. Kitty has an annoying habit
of not being alert to unauthorized hands—friends, friends of
friends, or hard-up housemates. Use an envelope entrusted to the
house bookkeeper if you have to use cash.

Back up a moment to the mysterious shopper. Who you elect
to make the weekly or bi-weekly shopping trip may depend upon
who has a car. If you own a car and are unwilling to loan it, then you

should willingly take on the duty or "privilege" of shopping. If several members own cars, then put shopping up on the chore wheel. Some house have only one shopper for other reasons. Terry, owner of a group house of eight people (famous among their acquaintances for their gourmet meals), is the only housemate who doesn't like to cook. So, he waives his cooking duty for shopping.

Shopping Tips

The group shopper should always go to the supermarket, co-op, or specialty store with a list in hand. Some groups have housemates give the shopper a list of ingredients they'll need for their meal that week. This method tends to be short-lived since it's hard to round up people and plan things in advance. A more sensible "no-fuss" way to shop is described by Brian, a solar contractor who is the unspoken leader of his politically active house in Philadelphia:

> We decide everything by consensus—even what we'll eat. At the beginning, we sat down and made a list of common things we eat to find out what everyone's diet is really like and what to buy when we shop cooperatively. We came up with this list. Before a shopping trip we circle what we need, what's running low. [See example 4.1]

This plan involves some haggling at the beginning but eliminates weekly menu collecting.

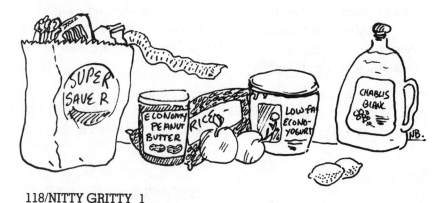

Example 4.1 -- Group House Grocery List

STAPLES

White Flour
Whole Wheat Flour
Baking Powder
Baking Soda
Cooking Oil
Cornstarch
Eggs
Mayonnaise
Mustard
Salad Dressing
Vinegar
Spices
Salt
Pepper
Brown Sugar
White Sugar
Honey
Tea
Coffee
Orange Juice (frozen)

DAIRY PRODUCTS

Butter
Margarine
Cheese
 - Mozzarella
 - Cream
 - Muenster
 - Cottage
 - Cheddar
Milk
Sour Cream
Yogurt

PRODUCE

Apples
Bananas
Grapefruit
Lemons
Oranges
Green Beans
Broccoli
Carrots
Celery
Cucumbers
Garlic
Lettuce
 - Romaine
 - Iceberg
 - Boston

PRODUCE

Onions
 - Yellow
 - Red
Peas (frozen)
Spinach
Potatoes
Tomatoes
Zucchini

BAKED GOODS

Bread
 - Rye
 - Wheat
 - Pumpernickel
 - Pocket
 - French
English Muffins
Hamburger Rolls
Cookies (!)

CANNED GOODS

Fruits
Fruit Juices
Tuna Fish
Vegetables
Soups

MEATS & FISH

Chicken
 - Parts
 - Whole
Hamburger Meat
Stew Meat
Lamb
Fish
Bacon
Sausage

MISCELLANEOUS

Peanut Butter
Jam, Jelly
Pickles
Nuts
Olives
Deli Foods
Soda
Rice
Pasta

HOUSEHOLD SUPPLIES

Dishwashing Liquid
Sponges, Dish Towels
Foil, Plastic Wrap
Furniture Polish
Laundry Detergent
Light Bulbs
Paper Bags
Paper Towels
Soap
Toilet Tissue
Window Cleaner

LIQUOR & LUXURIES

Beer
Wine
Gin
Scotch
Mixers
Ice Cream
_____
_____
_____
_____

Then there's the "bits and pieces" method of sharing food costs. One member will go out and get stuff for his meal and other things he likes, other members will do the same, and all put their receipts up on the bulletin board. At the end of the month, they add up the bills. Those who paid less reimburse those who paid more, or those who paid more earn a rent or utility credit. Though you might save time by not having to confer with housemates before shopping, the "bits and pieces" method won't save you money. Most people will shop on their way home from work or class without a glance or a thought as to what's in the communal cupboard. You may end up having duplicates or losing money by buying small quantities. In addition to the drawback of being uneconomical, this shopping method can bring on the "who bought what and why?" syndrome. Ed's student house in Morgantown, West Virginia, is a perfect example of a successful food sharing arrangment that deteriorated because of faulty mechanics:

> A conflict arose when we'd tally up the money for an entire two-week period. We'd see who was the high person and who was the low one, and we'd divide up the differences so they'd all equal out. Sometimes we'd rate people—who spent the most and who spent the least. There'd be a certain amount of pressure not to be the one who spent the most. If I went out and made a whole meal for six on only $22 and someone else went out and spent $45, I'd think why the hell! For only one meal, why is it going to cost me more?

One of the housemates took the goal of frugality too far, and Ed went on to describe what could only happen in a group house:

> Once Eric cooked this incredibly boring meal, rice and chicken livers. He only made them because they were .69 a pound. By this time what we were doing is you pay for the meal you cooked period. All things that did not go into the meal, you paid for separately. The idea

being that if you were an economical cook and could make a good meal for $15, why should you have to buy when someone else spent $30. Anyway Eric was always *cutting corners. He probably spent about $3 on a meal for four people. Bill came in from class, and when he saw the chicken livers, I thought he was going to punch Eric. It was comical because they were screaming 'chicken livers' back and forth. . . .*

A simple way to circumvent this problem is to agree to an amount, plus or minus $5.00, to spend on the group meal. And, while you are agreeing to things, you may want to discuss pros and cons of various shopping sources (see Advanced Group Living: Scene 3).

Food Sharing Philosophies and Practicalities

More important than consensus on how much to spend is an attitude toward the potential inequities of meal sharing—days out of town, dinner guests, larger appetites—things that can transform happy group consumers into vindictive itemizers. Indeed, if there were a prophet of group living, these are the words he would speak upon his visitation to a meal-sharing house, "Believe that it will all even out." Whether or not things do, in fact, exactly even out, households that don't examine every cent spent and whose mouth it fed will enjoy more harmonious relations than households with an itemizing eye. Ken, a thirty-year-old lawyer is a member/owner of a "believing" household. He said:

> *If one person has two guests in one week, no one makes any noise about it or asks that person to pay extra because everyone will have friends over for dinner at some point. We feel the same about missed meals. It just doesn't pay to haggle over dollars and cents in light of the big bonus we're getting by splitting the bill!*

All of Ken's five housemates share his sentiments, and that's the key; everyone has "gotta believe" for this philosophy to work.

Remember when you played tag and could yell "electricity," join hands with the other players, and "it" would be powerless against you? The same principle applies here, except "it" is the human tendency to look out for number one and number one only.

Of course there's nothing wrong with looking out for your concerns. Many meal-sharing groups take pains to account for all inequities. They don't just believe everything will equal out, they know it. If people in your house want to feel free to miss meals and to invite a guest for dinner without feeling as if they are losing out, or taking advantage of the others, you can devise ways to give people credit for nights spent away or to charge a set amount if they have more than an agreed upon minimum of guests for the month. The most simple way to account for guests/absences is shown in Example 4.2. You find out the cost for meals per day and then multiply that amount by the number of meal days each member has used to find the amount each person owes or is due at the end of the month (or two-week period).

Example 4.2: Simple Accounting System for Meal Cost/Use.
For December:

	Tom	Lynn	Jim	Janis	Total
Amt. Spent:	$20	$30	$22	$35	$107
Meal days used:	22	29	15	10	76
Amt. incurred:	$30.98	$40.88	$21.12	$14.08	at 107/76 or $1.40
owes or is due:	− $10.98	− $10.83	+ $ .88	− $20.92	per meal day

The Fairest Bookkeeping System in the Land

If you want to use what Dominique's household calls " the fairest bookkeeping system," get out your calculators and look at Example 4.3. Whew! Actually, their system isn't all that complex and has kept Dominique's five-member house financially and emotionally afloat for two years. In effect, everyone pays for the exact number of *food units* they have used during the month instead of *meal days*. The total food units for a month are calculated on the basis of breakfasts (1 unit each), and dinners (3 units each) as follows:

Breakfast	*1 unit x 5 people x 30 days*	*150 units*
Dinner	*3 unit x 5 people x 30 days*	*450 units*
	Total for the month	600 units

House members tally how much each has spent on food (also household goods); they total them; then divide the total cost by the number of units in the month (600) to get the cost of one meal unit. Each member then adds up food units for days away or dinners out and subtracts units for guests in or lunches taken in (2 units each). The resulting number of units is added to, or subtracted from, the total units allowed each member (120). The amount each member incurs for the month is each's unit total multiplied by the meal unit cost. For example, if Dominique incurred 113 food units at 75¢ each, her meal share for the month would be $84.75. If she spent $92, she would get a credit of $7.25. If she only spent $81.50, she would owe $3.25. Mechanical as this system is, it leaves absolutely no room for the ambiguities about food bills that cause so many major household disputes.

If you've decided to split the grocery bill and enjoy the communal fare, then "Bon Appetit!" Most people who share meals, for however long or short a time, look back nostalgically at those dinners where food, merriment, and dirty dishes abounded. Polly, a divorcee who lived in a group house until she remarried, lapses into reverie when she says:

> *Nothing was more pleasurable than coming home to a group of people I cared about, sitting down, and eating together, drinking wine, talking, even arguing. In the winter, we'd have coffee afterwards and sit by the fireplace. Now my daughter misses those times and she gets tired of my cooking.*

Example 4.3 --- The Fairest Bookkeeping System in the Land

$$30 \times 1 \times 5 = 150$$
$$30 \times 3 \times 5 = 450$$
$$\overline{600} \text{ meal units}$$

	Anne	Dominique	Joe	Paul	Karen	House Totals
Groceries	$3.00 6.65	$80.00 20.20 5.26	$50.19 21.00	$42.15 23.04 18.00	$36.00 31.40 29.00	
Food Total	$9.65	$105.46	$71.19	$83.19	$96.40	365.89 488 ≅ .75 (488 is Total meal units for house minus absences and guests -- 112) 365.89/600 ≅ .61 full house
Days Out (4 units)	ͲͲͰ ͲͲͰ	ͲͲͰ		||||	|	
Day Total	-40	-20	0	-16	-4	
Dinner Out (3 units)	ͲͲͰ ||||	ͲͲͰ ͲͲͰ	ͲͲͰ	ͲͲͰ ||||	ͲͲͰ |	
Dinner Total	-27	-30	-15	-27	-18	
Guests B(1) In L(2) D(3)	....	.... ͲͲͰ ͲͲͰ |	.... | ||	.... |	....	
Guest Total	0	+33	+8	+2	0	
Lunches In or Taken (2 units)	||||	|||		||	ͲͲͰ ͲͲͰ ||	
Lunch Total	+8	+6	0	+4	+24	
Meal Unit Total (MUT)	120 - 59 61	120 - 11 109	120 - 7 113	120 - 37 83	120 + 2 122	600 -112 488
Dollars Incurred (MUT x $/MU)	example: 61 x .75 = 45.74	$81.73	$84.73	$62.23	$91.47	
Dollars Incurred - Amt. Spent	45.74 - 9.65	$81.73 -105.46	$84.73 71.19	$62.23 - 83.19	$91.47 -96.40	
Amt. Due	-$36.09	+$23.73	-$13.54	+$20.06	+$4.93	

Collective Purchasing Sans Collective Eating

When you can't coordinate schedules in your house, then share the food bill without sharing meals. That way you can still reap the economic rewards of cooperative buying, you won't be expected home for dinner every night, and you can arrange communal dinners as you want them. Further, wildly different diets or preferences can be accomodated—provided, of course, that you "believe it all evens out."

Lenny, a political organizer from San Francisco and a group house veteran of eight years, still waxes enthusiastic about collective purchasing. Members of Lenny's house came up with a list of foods they ate. It features items like Twinkies, Ho Hos, and Doritos for a housemate who subsisted on junk food; sprouts, mung beans, and tofu for the house's "pseudo-veggie health-food types"; and wine, Pop-Tarts, steak, and canned green beans for everyone else. They xeroxed their eclectic grocery list and circled items as they needed them:

> *There was absolutely everything. Our house was like a supermarket. Being in a well-stocked house and enjoying that communal surplus gives you such a fantastic feeling. If you wanted to have ten people over for dinner on the spur of the moment, you could do it without shopping first.*

One thing to watch out for, there's more concern about big and small appetites, expensive and less expensive tastes in houses that share food bills. When you don't consume together, you might begin to assume instead—people *assume* that everyone else is eating more than their share. If you find yourself spending more time eyeing the refrigerator shelves than eating what's on them, stand back a moment to assess whether the inequity perceived is just a distortion or really something to be concerned about. Distortion, for example, is when you begrudge a housemate her taste for expensive Pepperidge Farm cookies while turning a blind eye to your own insistence that there always be a six pack of Perrier in the refrigerator. Chances are something else is bothering you, and the cookies are a convenient foil.

On the other hand—in group living there is *always* another hand—if you are a lone herbivore living among carnivores, a lone dieter among carefree skinnies, or a lone budgeter among spendthrifts, speak up or forever hold your peace. Instead of hassling with prorating the food expenses to accomodate your diet or wallet, bring up the inequity as a point of discussion at a house meeting or at a time when everyone happens to be gathered together. You might be able to convince your house to move to the next arrangement on the group house food spectrum.

Stable Staple Sharing

The most sensible arrangement you can have if too many real or perceived injustices crop up when you split the food bill is to share only the staples—the food you eat in common. Write a list of all the things you want to buy together. Post this "house needs" list and next to it a sheet labeled "house expenses." Whenever someone buys orange juice or eggs, for instance, they just write in what they spent on the "house expenses" sheet, cross the item out on the "house needs" list, and at the end of the month all expenses are charged to housemates.

Make sure you all talk about what everyone considers to be staples before you buy something and put it on the house expenses sheet. Though Lily's household consumes gallons of wine monthly, the housemates don't buy wine together. "Tina and I drink better wines than the rest of the house. I wouldn't think of drinking Carlo Rossi, while the others would," Lily said. If you and your housemates start to squabble over whether to buy Hellmann's mayonnaise or Brand X, you know it's time to seriously consider switching to the next arrangement. . . .

Going Dutch

Open the refrigerator in Donna's house, and here is what you might see: five cartons of milk with varying expiration dates (one in the farthest corner even predates pasteurization) and covered with curious hieroglyphics. Lining the inside of the door are rows of eggs, some monogrammed. On the second shelf are four loaves of bread ranging in color from pumpernickel brown to Wonder Bread white to bread-mold blue. The third shelf sports a more colorful array of plastic containers bearing labels like "Donna's spaghetti, Do not touch under penalty of law." Lastly, in the vegetable crispers, someone has personalized three parsnips and a flaccid stalk of celery with masking tape.

This is an extreme case, but believe it or not, redundancy in the refrigerator and personalized parsnips make good sense to many households that purchase all food items separately. Some say that keeping separate grocery tabs is more practical. While it is far from being economically practical, it can be instrumental in maintaining good house karma. For example, in group houses whose members are virtual strangers and who came together for economic convenience rather than compatability, purchasing items collectively would be giving their group more structure and cohesiveness than they're willing to have.

Still others see the dutch treat arrangement as a last resort. Like people who have been burned in past love relationships, they say "never again" to food sharing. Lise, a financially secure flight attendant, remembered her first group house with this kind of bitterness, "I was on a diet, so I would subsist for weeks on cottage cheese, yogurt, and vegetables, but I ended up paying for everyone else's hamburger meat and junk food. Now, in my new place, we keep everything separate. . . . It's the best way to do it."

Whatever reasons prompt you and your housemates to "go your own way" regarding groceries, it helps to keep these basic guidelines in mind:

- If you've got one refrigerator and more than five people (or fewer people with hearty appetites), consider buying an additional refrigerator. One household bought an old refrigerator for $10.00, but it was worth ten times that much since it restored sanity in their kitchen.
- If there is enough cupboard and refrigerator space, divide it up among you. If not, label your food. Try not to get too elaborate or threatening on your labels. A simple piece of tape with your name or initials on it will suffice. We heard about a medical student at Johns Hopkins who labeled containers "CAUTION: bacteriological specimen, do not open." One day, a housemate got curious and opened it, only to find some leftover macaroni and cheese. Don't squander your creativity in the refrigerator!

An efficient household in Boston came up with a labeling technique worthy of imitation. They bought those little colored stick-on dots at a stationery store and had everyone choose a color. Whatever wasn't dotted was considered communal. The dots were especially helpful for labeling ambiguous foil packets in the freezer.

- *Never, ever,* eat anyone else's food without asking.
- If you do eat a housemate's food (while drunk after a party or sleep-eating), don't leave a poetic apology taped on the 'fridge. Tell the owner and offer to replace it. Then replace it . . . as soon as you can.
- If you notice minimal amounts of your own food missing (your peanut butter is glopped in a different formation than when you last scooped), count to ten and say to yourself, Is it that big a deal? The answer will probably be no.

- If large quantities of your food keep disappearing and you don't know who the culprit is, discuss the matter with the whole house. If you do know who is taking your food, confront that person alone without dragging in the whole house. Refrain from writing notes that say, "Somebody's eating my food," when you know very well who that "body" is.

These rules may become unneccessary after a while. As you loosen up and get to know each other, you stop being on guard, you share a meal with housemate, and she, in turn, cooks for you. Before you know it, you are food sharers. This happened in Bill's group house in west Philadelphia where the housemates are collective eaters rather than collective buyers. "We know what we can and can't take of each other's food. Unwritten rules develop. If someone buys a big expensive cut of meat and tucks it into the back of the freezer, you just don't take it out and thaw it." That kind of common sense and courtesy is invaluable in all aspects of group living, but especially so when you want to enjoy going dutch.

Good Group Housekeeping

When you have five people living under one roof, what happens when it's time to clean the floor? The kitchen? The bathrooms? The seemingly mundane matter of housecleaning and how it's apportioned is of supreme importance to the well being of every group house. In interviews, when the talk turned to group housekeeping, a terminology began to materialize. The words *threshold* and *tolerance level* kept popping up as in, "You know, my last housemate had a low—a very low—threshold for messiness. I mean he was always getting after me to clean this or clean that." Or, "Ellen and I had a pretty high tolerance level for filth, which didn't make Robert and Joanne very happy." As part of your initiation into the truly singular world of cleaning plurally, study the "Guide" to a few extremes on the tolerance continuum.

A Guide to Group House Cleaning Types

The Neat-Nik. Not to be confused with people who wear black turtleneck sweaters, shades, and berets, neat-niks are known for their "cleaner than thou," posture. Neat-niks can't stand the sight of anything astray, ajar, or akimbo. Cleaning gives them a feeling of control over their own world and that of their housemates as they hold the broom over them. Neat-niks do not last long in group houses.

Therapeutic Cleaners. These people get "in touch with their feelings" through cleaning. When "dealing with anger," they're likely to scrub the pots so hard the enamel comes off. Other than little mishaps like that, therapeutic cleaners are a bonus in any house. Beware! Manic-depressive cleaners can suddenly revert to a state of extreme slovenliness until a whiff of Mr. Clean gets them to rush for the mop and bucket.

"Joan of Arc" Cleaners. You know them. They feel it is their duty to clean up after everyone else. Sometimes they will start cleaning the oven at the most absurd times just to circumvent someone else's good intentions—you wonder if they have fantasies of being accidentally gassed in the line of duty. You'll come downstairs in the morning to slip on the still wet Mop-and-Glowed floor. After you recover, you say in surprise, "Oh, you did the floor, it looks great but *I* was gonna do it today." "OOOOOH it was nothing," says Joan of Arc (or John of Arc), sipping her morning coffee, bags under her eyes from this most admirable cleaning stint.

The Closet Slob. These people are very responsible in the communal areas and don't bother others about their cleaning habits or lack thereof.

The closet slob will appear to be at the median point in the tolerance continuum until you notice him sleeping on the living room couch five nights in a row. Knowing that no one is occupying his room, you ask if perhaps the bathtub or roof is leaking above his room. "No," he blushes. One day, curiousity kills the housemate, and you open the door to his bedroom to be swallowed in an avalanche of newspapers, clothes, Nip-chee cracker wrappers, books, records, coffee cups, ad infinitum. You have just encountered the closet slob's secret stash.

The Lovable Slob.

This forlorn creature has the habit of leaving remnants of himself all over the house. His signature is a pile of dirty dishes in the sink, footprints in the bathtub, crumbs on the table, socks in the hallway. He mumbles apologetically when anyone meekly requests, "Could you, um, try, um, to be a little, um, neater?" He promises sincerely to do better as he ambles to his bedroom. Then you pick up his jacket, books, coffee cup, or half-eaten sandwich—and sigh.

The Social Change Slob.

As abrasive as the lovable slob is humble, this housemate tries to convince the others that her particular messiness is a political statement. She might feel that the purest form of anarchy is to "live and make mess." Or, she may see herself as a champion for filth. Instead of a soap box, the social change slob will use a trashcan as her speaking platform. She'll even boycott soap suds because she seeks to create a more habitable environment for downtrodden cockroaches. Like neat-niks, social change slobs do not last long in group houses.

Probably none of these types will be present in your house in their "pure" form, but in the history of group living, those with neat-nik tendencies seem destined to share quarters with those who exhibit slob impulses. From the array of mess-thresholds, your group's task will be to find a common standard of cleanliness. One household's common standard was succinctly expressed in the description of their house as "messy but clean."

Keeping a house from being "messy" requires the conscientious day-by-day efforts of individuals, such as picking things up as you go and not leaving your stuff around. Keeping your house "clean" will require a group effort. Without some kind of cleaning system, housemates might direct gripes toward each other, often hurtfully. "*You're* so sloppy, I always have to pick up after you." Or, "Why do you keep coming after me with a sponge, for God's sake! Are you trying to be my mother or something? You have some kind of complex? In my psych 101 class, they say . . . " With a system, you can direct complaints, suggestions, or rebuttals back to the written agreement. "Hey, it's your turn to do the bathroom. Did you forget?" Or "It doesn't specify that cleaning the oven is part of cleaning the kitchen so I didn't do it." Housemates then start working toward the goal of keeping the house clean and not of one-upping each other.

Another bonus of having a written agreement is that it, and not your housemates, will remind you when it is chore time. The danger of going without a cleaning system is that housemates will harbor their own expectations of others' duties—little contracts—in their heads. When a housemate unknowingly violates the contract, the result is tension.

To further alleviate the inevitable tension over discrepancies in cleaning standards, the ability to *compromise* is an absolute necessity. Compromising involves trying to understand the people you live with, putting yourself in their place rather than putting them in their place. Alan, an easygoing artist who shares a house with three others, described himself as "tidy and meticulous." Yet he conceded:

Every person I meet teaches me something new. There are times when it's important not to wash their dishes because they want to live in an atmosphere that's a little bit untidy. That's an atmosphere that they built for themselves. And my going in and cleaning up after them sometimes creates in people a sense of guilt and resentment instead of a feeling of appreciation. So, in a way, I say to myself, It's really selfish of me to think that I must go and tidy up after people.

Talking about your expectations of each other and trying to figure out how you can meet them, if only halfway, will help keep those unspoken unsigned contracts from ever forming.

The "Let it Evolve" Theory of Housecleaning

Despite all the glories of the cleaning system, this chapter would be incomplete without mentioning the non-system approach that a good many group houses advocate. Groups that adhere to the "let it evolve" theory of housecleaning believe that chores should not be assigned but that cleaning roles evolve naturally in the course of life together. Lenny, whose San Francisco group house was actually a mansion that demanded frequent cleaning, said:

We talked over the years about having a rotation of duties, but gradually we came to accept the idea that people do what they like to do. It's very difficult and usually destructive to fellowship in the house to set up rotation. Some people like to do windows, others, the kitchen floor and cleaning the refrigerator, while some are obsessive about cleaning toilets.

Not only do "people do what they like to do," reasons another group dweller who found rotation repugnant, but *people do what* they are best at doing. In Leo's Portland, Oregon, group house, those who favored cleaning the windows were more "skilled" at window-washing, while the housemate who gravitated toward the bathroom usually had a flair with the toilet brush.

Although it's uplifting to think of chores as skills and talents instead of drudgery, the majority of those who "let it evolve" concede that housemates' hidden "talents" for floor mopping or shelf dusting often remain hidden. Further, resentment cropped up between the sexes in co-ed houses as women became bathroom cleaners by default and men were held responsible for the yardwork. Lastly, the people who are home the most and who have to look at the messes often evolve into house drudges rather than cheerful cleaners.

In households that did function well without assigning duties, either all housemates had the same cleanliness standards, or they stringently followed two golden rules for group living. In fact *everyone*, regardless of how loose or rigid their housecleaning structure, should try to follow these two edicts; your life together will be much simpler.

Two Golden Rules

1. Clean up after yourself in the kitchen.
2. Pick your own hairs out of the bathtub or sink.

If you think that it takes too much time to rinse out a coffee cup or go over the counter with a sponge, you're fooling yourself. It takes much more time to clean a stack of dirty dishes or a week's accumulation of grit in the bathroom than the minute or two it will take you to do these things right then and there. When everyone makes a concerted effort to leave things as they find them, the result is, "...like magic. You've got this big facility, this kitchen ready to go, and you can be your most creative and most hospitable."

Assigning Your Homework

When it comes to assigning chores, the word "homework" instead of "housework" sounds more hospitable. After all, your goal in cleaning is to make your group house more habitable, a place you want to come *home* to. It's true that living in a grand mansion creates more incentive for cleaning than living in your typical "in need of repair" group house, but making and keeping an ordinary place clean and attractive can do a lot to strengthen the ties among a group of disparate individuals. When this basic level of interaction is established, it is much easier to establish bonds on more complex levels.

Now that you have a positive outlook on cleaning (Ha!), you can decide with your housemates which areas need periodic cleaning, how tasks will be distributed among yourselves, and how often these jobs should be done. Try to balance the work equally among housemates. Task distribution will probably be a function of how many people you have. If you've got seven people and only four tasks, don't make up three piddly things for the other three to do. When the number of chores and people don't even out, give some housemates "time off" each week or divide into two-housemate cleaning teams. Two people might tackle the trash, two others, the kitchen, and two more, the bathrooms. Teams are especially practical in a large house in which cleaning a week's worth of kitchen mess might be too overwhelming for one person. Also, try to be specific about what each task entails; better yet, put the details in writing. It may sound ridiculous to catalog scientifically each component of kitchen duty, for instance, but remember: little misunderstandings often spark the biggest house blow-ups, usually because people think some things are too trivial to make explicit.

Deciding how often each chore should be done can be a source of friction in group houses. Don, an environmental researcher whose household was composed of people at opposite ends of the tolerance scale, told how chores weren't getting done at all because of the unrealistic expectations imposed by the house "neat-niks." The messy contingent rebelled against having to do chores more often than they felt was necessary, and resentment built up when the tidy majority began cleaning up after them, even when something wasn't their assigned task. Steve, one of the more lax members, said:

> We finally decided on the cleaning plan I had always advocated. We decided on the minimum amount of times something should get done. For instance, we're going to vacuum the house at least once every two weeks instead of once a week like we had it before. That's just a minimum—you could do it more, but as long as someone's done their minimum, they're off the hook, and . . . Don's free to clean up after them.

You'd be wise to follow the example of Don's household and work out an arrangment that suits the temperament of your particular household instead of deciding on arbitrary chore "due dates."

Don and Steve's house, as you can see by their cleaning chart (Example 4.4), is one in which each member has a task that they do for long stretches of time. Although it may be depressing to contemplate cleaning the bathroom every other week for a year, fixed duties allow more freedom for those with hectic schedules—there's one less thing to hassle with. Also, assigning fixed duties is a natural follow up to a "let it evolve" arrangement. Everyone still does the chores they prefer, only now it is "official." The drawback is that someone inevitably gets a raw deal, like the person who has to take out the trash, a chore which must be done almost every day. Also, sexual pigeonholing in co-ed houses becomes more of a danger when tasks are not rotated.

Example 4.4: Cleaning Chart (Fixed Duties)

Bathroom (& Bilk) — Don
Kitchen — Jim
Garbage & cans downstairs — Beth
Vacuuming — Steve
Kitchen Floor — Elizabeth

✓ oh, Boy, I'm Done!

oh, Boy, no chore that week

WEEK OF: TASK:	Jan 24-30	Feb 31-6	Feb 7-13	Feb 14-20	Feb 21-27	March 28-6	March 7-13	March 14-20	March 21-27
	▨		✓		▨		▨		
	▨	✓			▨		▨		▨
	✓	✓	✓	▨	▨		▨	wash can	
	▨			▨			▨	▨	▨
	▨	✓	▨	▨					▨

Round and Round and Round She Goes, Where She Stops . . . God Only Knows

Rotation of house duties is, in short, the only way to ensure even distribution of the work. Whether you rotate tasks weekly, bi-weekly, or once a month (for the sluggish among you), you can draw up a grid chart (Example 4.5) *or* make a workwheel (Example 4.6) to stick on the fridge or bulletin board. Workwheels are much more inspiring than charts, however. Just imagine the excitement each week when you get to turn the wheel one more notch, housemates breathlessly awaiting their next chore. Furthermore, workwheels don't resemble the bureaucratic forms we encounter daily in our jobs or academic life: A mere spin of the wheel harkens back to elementary school days when it was finally our turn to do the erasers. Another nifty thing about the workwheel is that its form is symbolic of the very best in group living: the wheel stands for progress and motion, the circle for unity, and everyone's pie-slice for the individuality coupled with responsibility that makes the wheel turn—however painstakingly. As Bob, an editor in a Brooklyn Heights brownstone, said:

> *Sometimes it takes two weeks to get them all done. If the majority of the chores are done, the wheel is turned. Dan was very busy with two jobs for a while, and he didn't have a lot of time, so often his jobs didn't get done. Eileen is busy at school and with her kids, so sometimes hers didn't get done for a little bit. That came up at one of the meetings . . . but it's working. Last week everyone had done their chores, and there was some astonishment over that.*

In fact, one house actually threw a party to celebrate the rare occasion when everyone's jobs were done on time. It was, by all accounts, a glorious bash. Then, there are those reckless moments when, for a lark the house decides to forgo all systems and spin the wheel as if it were a roulette machine in Atlantic City, no one knowing what the result will be. Some houses do this on a regular basis with the members taking bets on where their names ended up. We even heard of one group that raised $300 that way in the course of a year. Needless to say, they spent the money on a maid. Wouldn't you?

Dealing with the Unholy Mess

You've let it evolve, assigned duties, made a workwheel out of orange and blue sheets of construction paper, and still your house cannot join forces on the cleaning issue. The workwheel doesn't turn, or if it does, it turns backwards, and people are sparring with each other over picayune things. Perhaps you live in a house where everyone has a hectic schedule—flight attendants, executives, graduate students, and people who work the graveyard shift—and you really don't have time to tidy up the communal areas. Before the next crumb falls from the table to join its friends on the floor and your landlord declares your house a health hazard, ask yourselves; is it worth the sanity of all concerned to hire *someone else* to do the dirty work? In other words, it may be time to hire a maid. A maid? You may be shocked to learn that a number of groups hire maids or "household technicians" as they are now androgynously called. Not only households that dine on caviar seek outside help, but those that subsist on "tuna tempter" as well. Having a maid today will cost about $45 for a weekly visit. Dividing that among you could be considered cheap, and think of the rewards—the only housework your group will have to do is the dishes!

There are still people for whom having an outsider come in and clean goes against their principles, against their wallets, or against their insecurity about having the dusty corners of their lives exposed to a stranger. If you and your house want a break from the housecleaning routine, either make cleaning an occasion,

Example 4.5: Rotating Chore Chart

May Cleaning Schedule

	1 - 7	8 - 14	15 - 21	22 - 28
Robert	Kitchen	trash/recycling	living room/plants	bathroom
Ellen	bathroom	Kitchen	trash/recycling	living room/plants
Peter	living rm/plants	bathroom	Kitchen	trash/recycling
Kathy	trash/recycling	living room/plants	bathroom	Kitchen

Kitchen— clean range, counters, table, refrigerator, sweep floor and mop.

Bathroom— clean sink, tub, toilet, sweep floor and mop.

living room/plants — vacuum rug, dust shelves and tables, water plants all through the house.

trash/recycling— take trash out on Tuesdays and Fridays. take papers and aluminum cans to recycler.

Example 4.6: The Workwheel

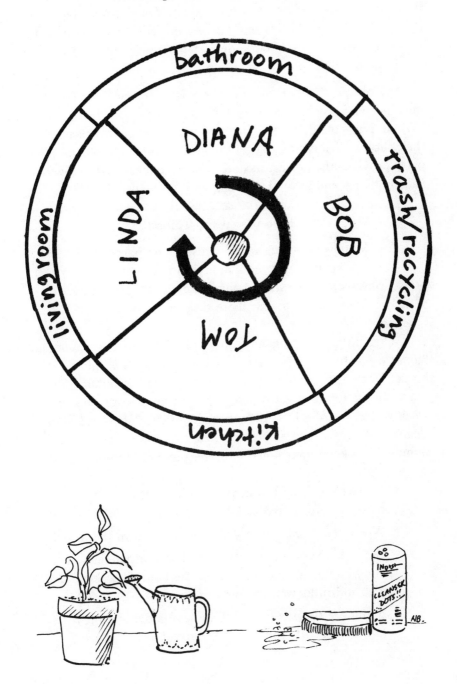

or make an occasion for cleaning. The first alternative involves making cleaning day into a party of sorts. You buy a couple of six packs, blast the music, invite a few masochistic friends over, wash the windows, wax the floors, defrost the refrigerator, set up the roach motels, and so on.

More houses favor making an occasion for cleaning (i.e., having a party). Esther, a secretary for a public relations firm, told us, "When things would be slipping for a while and people slack off on their chores, the best way to get things done was to have a party." A party provides the perfect incentive, and the mess that follows can usually be packed into a Hefty bag within a half hour.

Those Disgusting Things

Mildew on sponges and whiskers on porcelain,
Lint in the dryer, a mouse in the kitchen,
Newspapers we should have thrown out last spring,
These are a few of those disgusting things . . .

This ditty could be any group dweller's lament about all "those disgusting things"—mold, dust, roaches—that inhabit their house. While the communal areas of group houses (kitchen, living room and bathrooms) get divvied up between housemates for the weekly cleaning, the little daily practices that really *keep* a house clean tend to go ignored. Here, then, are some tips, rules, and reminders to keep your house from becoming a dump.

- If there's a little trap in your bathtub drain that catches hairs, clean it periodically.
- When you shave, wash your whiskers down the drain.
- Get a double-layered shower curtain that you can drape along the inside and outside of the bathtub to keep puddles and mildew from forming.
- If you are fortunate enough to have a dryer, empty the lint trap each time you use the dryer.

- Keep old newspapers off the furniture and in a neat stack out of everyone's way. Better yet, throw them away each week or recycle them.
- When the spirit moves you to clean, pay attention to oft-neglected hallways and what one man called "traffic areas": the wall space around light switches that always gets smudged by groping fingers.
- Consider going without shoes if there is a lot of traffic in your house. Shoe-less houses are viewed by some as quasi-religious, but they are practical: you keep grit and grime outside where it belongs, cut down on noise, and are forced to clean your socks more often!
- Take out the trash without fail. It's amazing how an over-full trashcan will suddenly take over the whole kitchen while the stench of week-old trash takes over your whole house.
- Don't let plates, glasses, and mugs collect in your room. One woman we heard about was trying to make a wedding dowry, but gave the house roaches instead.
- Don't put empty bottles or containers back in the refrigerator. Clean them out, or throw them out.
- Assign defrosting the fridge as a monthly chore. You might have a night or week when you and your housemates use up all of the food in the freezer. Frozen peas, ice cream, and Mrs. Paul's fishsticks make an unusual casserole.
- Check periodically for moldy food in the fridge. In this instance, you *are* your housemates' keeper. Throw out anything that looks suspicious.
- Keep extra grease cans by the stove.
- After washing the dishes, wring out the sponge. When you literally "throw in the sponge" it gets mildewed.
- Laugh whenever you can.

Do Women in Group Houses End Up Doing the Dirty Work?

Do any of these reports sound familiar?

I sometimes feel the men who live in this house are serviced by the women. They have a great deal. John's gone shopping twice. That was when I made him come with me. The other two have never shopped for food. John's cooked about two meals. (Suzanne, twenty-eight, graphic designer)

The women ended up doing most of the cooking. I don't know, they just enjoyed doing it, and hey, I'm not complaining. If they want to do the cooking, fine. I'll sit down and read the paper. (Mark, twenty-four, dental student)

I don't want to live with three men because three men are going to be slobs. . . . The women I see are leaning more in the direction of domesticity, and I want to capitalize on it. Hopefully, I too, will become more and more domestic for my own good. (Frank, twenty, congressional intern)

In the house where I live in now—two women and four men—Eva and I are the ones who always do the bathroom, mop the floors, and clean the dishes! (Patty, thirty, restaurant manager)

If Charles Dickens were alive to comment on the typical 1980s-style group house, he'd probably say, "It was the most liberated of times. It was the least liberated of times." Nowadays, men and women have few qualms about sharing quarters.

Everything's cool until the issue of housecleaning is broached. There are exceptions, but it appears that women tend to do more than their share of the "dirty work," so much so that women who move in with two or more men risk becoming live-in maids. When men leave messes and women pick them up, both are fulfilling the patterns in which they were brought up. You can think of housecleaning as a skill that most men never learned, just as women weren't taught the strategies for getting ahead in the business world that men seem to know intuitively.

What better place than a group house for unlearning those old stereotypes and learning new skills. That's the beauty of rotating chores. It is the only way that work can be distributed equally. Then the only bone of contention is how well people tackle their chores, and the cure for that problem is patience. Women should share their domestic know-how with men instead of needling them for a job undone or poorly done, just as men should reveal to women the intricacies of lawn mower repair. Don't resort to martyrdom, and try not to be patronizing to less domestic or less handy housemates.

Patty remembered how she came downstairs one morning and was shocked to see the previous night's stock of dirty dishes drying on the rack. Eva was out of town, she hadn't done them herself, and the male housemates had a history of avoiding the kitchen sink. On closer inspection she realized that there was a greasy film on all of the plates, spots on the glasses, and grit on the silverware. David, sitting cherubically in the living room, had forgotten to use soap. Patty, grateful yet practical, then attempted to wash all the dishes again *without* David knowing it. Since it's virtually impossible to wash dishes on the sly when someone's in the next room, David stormed in at the first clinks and clatters, incensed that his hard work whould go for naught. In a situation like this, it may be better to swallow a little grit and dispense a little humor to save hurt feelings. "Hey, David, thanks for doing the dishes, but next time use the Ivory."

Advanced Group Living: Scene 3, Supermarket Sweep: Cut Food Costs By Capitalizing on the Collective

For the same reasons you are drawn to the cooperative lifestyle—economy, companionship, and ideology—consider buying your food in a co-op or at a wholesale market. As a group, collective buying power is one of your greatest resources. Apply it to food, and you can easily reduce both the cost of your grocery list and the amount of time you spend shopping.

Depending, of course, on what you buy and when you buy it, you can save 50 percent or more of the price of many items. Bulk purchase of perishable produce is especially economical, one wholesaler explained, because stores actually charge you for the spoilage. However, supermarkets sell staples such as flour, sugar, and milk very close to cost, so you won't save much on these items.

If you favor an alternate lifestyle, you'll find the co-op not only a good place to shop but a congenial atmosphere where you're bound to meet like-minded people. Often the most complete listings for group houses are on the co-op bulletin board, and chances are you'll find the "food for people not for profit" philosophy appealing.

Almost every town has some kind of co-op or alternate food store, a makeshift affair in a low-rent area with a name like "The Fertile Earth," "Over the Rainbow" or "Fields of Plenty." Peek in the window, and you'll find a mix of people—bearded men with pony tails, women in worn overalls, kids, perhaps even a few patrons in three-piece suits. You'll find the shelves brimming with barrels of grains, dried beans, and whole-wheat macaroni; hearty fresh breads; butters from unlikely nuts; and organically grown produce, all blotchy and bruised as if to prove a point. And there are always the cheeses, the yogurt, the fresh tofu, and raw milk.

But even if you prefer to buy Rice-a-Roni and Sugar Pops at the Safeway, a trip to the co-op is worthwhile simply for the spices. By scooping them out of a jar and bagging them yourself, you can save five to ten times the cost of oregano, cinnamon, parsley, and many other exotic and obscure seasonings.

Some co-ops have work requirements, calling on members to contribute five to ten hours of their time a month, while others charge a membership fee. In return, you might get a ten to twenty percent discount on food that is already substantially cheaper than it is at the supermarket. By splitting the responsibility among your housemates, you can get the maximum return on the minimum investment of time and money, and what could be a more compelling argument for co-op shopping than that?

However, if you're really short on cash but long for an adventurous shopping experience, go straight to the source. Vickie, a journalist in Virginia who lives with two other women, set up a wholesale food buying group that is so efficient the members have to shop only twice a year. With her busy reporter's schedule, the fewer shopping trips the better.

"We rounded up several interested houses, about 25 people in all, which we think is the optimum number," she said. "It allows us to get a variety of foods in reasonable quantities that we can consume before it spoils." Shopping is done early Saturday morning once every three weeks in two-person units. Everybody pays a $6 share for produce the day before.

"The first thing we did was check the yellow pages for food brokers and wholesale suppliers," she explained. "Then we made a list of definite no-no's—the food everyone hates. Lima beans are about the only thing on it, although we're strongly polarized over brussels sprouts and artichokes."

The shopping team takes the money, usually about $120, to a produce market for fruits and vegetables and a dairy market for eggs, cheese, butter, milk, and poultry. Members make individual orders for dairy and pay for them separately, but they take pot luck on produce. "You have to be flexible about what you get," Vickie said. "We encourage people to buy the kinds of food they would normally get at the grocery store. But the emphasis is on seasonal food and the less expensive items. It means you might get spinach when you really wanted broccoli or two heads of lettuce when all you need is one, but it's worth it. Not only is the price low, but the quality is always excellent."

Of course, wholesale buying means bringing home 40 pounds of bananas, ten pounds of cheddar cheese, a box of 250 oranges, or a whole carton of asparagus. So be prepared to divide it up. You'll need paper and plastic bags, a good knife to cut the cheese, and a scale or yardstick to measure out portions of solid bulk items. Save your egg cartons, because wholesale eggs come in bulk lots of 15 dozen. Also, you'll need to take a notepad and calculator when you shop, or find a friend who is willing to lend fingers and toes to some particularly difficult computation. The process, from picking out the produce to picking up the packages may take five or six hours, but then again, you only have to do it once or twice a year.

Aside from the savings, buying wholesale is very convenient. Vickie said, "It may seem like a big production, but you don't have to be that organized. If you consider what you invest in time when you stop off at the supermarket twice a week, you can see what a big time saver shopping collectively is."

Supermarket, Co-op, and Wholesale Buying—The Pros and Cons

Supermarket

Convenience. Many supermarkets are open twenty-four hours a day, are in easy to reach locations and have parking facilities.

One-stop shopping. They have everything from lentils to lightbulbs.

Long lines at peak times.

Wide selection. Standard types of food, including meats.

Extensive offerings of prepared food. Supermarkets are the best places to buy canned, frozen, and pre-packaged food.

Always well-stocked.

Will take checks. Will cash checks.

Higher prices. Of course, you have to pay for the selection, the packaging and the convenience.

Co-op

Less convenient. Co-ops are often in out of the way spots, and you may have to bring your own bags, bottles and jars.

Two stop shopping. They often don't have much prepared food, unless it's some kind of vegetarian specialty, which is bound to be expensive. So you'll have to go to the supermarket for Twinkies and paper products. Also, most co-ops don't carry meat.

Lower prices. Dairy and produce is usually 10 to 20 cents a pound cheaper than in a supermarket. Nuts are about half price, and spices are a mere fraction of what they cost in a chain store.

Not always well-stocked. Inevitably, the co-op will be out of something you desperately need, but don't worry, they'll be getting a shipment in next week.

Good selection of alternate foods. For vegetarians, pepole with food allergies or on special diets, co-ops can be real lifesavers.

Greater time investment. You might have to work at the co-op five to ten hours a month, but chances are you'll meet some very interesting characters.

Ideology. Your money goes to maintain the co-op rather than into a profit-making business.

Wholesale Buying

Slightly less convenient. Wholesale buying involves a certain amount of research and planning in the beginning stages and then special trips to warehouses once the mechanism is rolling.

Extra work. Plan on devoting some time to dividing the produce and then packaging it for individual members. It may seem a formidable task, but you only have to do it once or twice a year.

Several-stop shopping. You usually have to go to one wholesaler for produce, one for dairy, and one for dry goods, as well as picking up processed food and paper products at a supermarket. However, you probably only need to do this once a month.

The lowest prices. You get substantial savings from buying in bulk. That's what supermarkets and restaurants do, so why not do it yourself. For example, a carton with 250 oranges in season costs about $12. Now that's economy.

Excellent quality. When you buy wholesale you get the first pick of absolutely fresh produce. This means it will last even longer once you get it home.

Ideology. Your money goes to the distributor and the farmer rather than to the supermarket companies.

Have to pay cash.

Dairy	Wholesale	Co-op	Supermarket
eggs	.76 doz.	1.37 doz. (organic)	.80 doz
cheddar cheese	2.25 lb.	3.65 lb.	3.69 lb.
Havarti	2.45 lb.	3.65 lb.	3.50 lb.
Jarlsburg	2.89 lb.	4.05 lb.	4.39 lb.
muenster	1.95 lb.	3.00 lb.	2.90 lb.
chicken breasts (boneless)	2.20 lb.	—	2.60 lb.

Produce			
broccoli	.70 lb.	.75 lb.	.89 lb.
carrots	.25 lb.	.40 lb.	.51 lb.
lettuce	.35 lb.	.40 lb.	.50 lb.
potatoes	.20 lb.	.20 lb.	.34 lb.
onions	.19 lb.	.20 lb.	.49 lb.
bananas	.30 lb.	.30 lb.	45 lb.
artichokes	.45 each	.85 each	.98 each

Grains, Nuts, Etc.			
brown rice	.69 lb.	.49 lb.	.73 lb.
split peas	.49 lb.	.55 lb.	1.43 lb.
lentils	.61 lb.	.61 lb.	.69 lb.
pancake mix	.62 lb.	.57 lb.	.72 lb.
cashews	4.88 lb.	5.20 lb.	7.44 lb.
almonds	3.59 lb.	3.20 lb.	6.32 lb.
raisins	1.37 lb.	1.60 lb.	1.70 lb.

Spices			
basil		.17 oz.	3.00 oz.
red pepper		.25 oz.	1.00 oz.
garlic salt		.22 oz.	.46 oz.
dill		.47 oz.	2.00 oz.
oregano		.21 oz.	2.40 oz.
parsley		.43 oz.	3.60 oz.

Group House Nitty Gritty II: Men and Women, Kids & Cats, Guests and Pests

Group houses were considered the sexual stomping grounds of the 1960s—the perfect setting for men and women to engage in carefree and spontaneous sexual liaisons. Now that free love, or at least free sex, is relatively easier to find on one's own, group houses have become the *testing* grounds for more rewarding albeit less passionate sonds. Housemates can enjoy a special relationship that is somewhere in the netherland between acquired sibling and friend. Some people expressed delight at recreating their family as they always wanted it to be. Said Don, a member of a household with three men and two women, "Our relationships are more like a brother/sister type thing. I grew up with two brothers, and I always wanted to have sisters . . . now I have two, Beth and Ellen." Unlike siblings, however, you can start from scratch with housemates, unblinded by the emotional fog of family ties.

The Plusses of Being Platonic

When men and women share quarters, their eyes are opened in a number of ways—sometimes quite literally, as when men get slapped by three pairs of wet pantyhose when they step into the shower or when women collapse onto a toilet with its seat left up. You'll see each other as fellow human beings and not solely as sex objects. This is when any sexual stereotypes you might hold gradually fade as more and more the men or women you live with don't conform to "the way you've always heard it should be." The insights gleaned from housemates of the opposite sex will be especially valuable for those venturing into the turbulent waters of a new love relationship or those (divorcees, for instance) who have "washed up on the shore."

Even with all the platonic potential, there are still going to be a lot of sexual "molecules" in the air when men and women share housing. This inevitable tension between the sexes is hard enough to deal with at the office, in classes, and elsewhere in daily life, so how do you respond (or rather, Do you respond?) when it's in your home. Even if housemates don't feel any surges of passion for each other, a delicate balance is disrupted when you've got people leaving and entering your household every so often. Once you have built up an immunity to the sexual vibes of Peter and Sam, they both move out and in walks a stranger named Jonathon with a flashing smile, penetrating eyes, and a penchant for washing dishes. This really happened in Donna's household. Donna, a graduate student at the University of Pennsylvania, lives with Celia and Ed, a married couple who own the house and feel it is their prerogative to choose new housemates. Their most recent find is Dennis, an excrutiatingly handsome manager of a construction firm (single to boot). Donna, who is at a very vulnerable period of her life and has a history of falling for handsome men, is wary about living with Dennis. "There's enough in my life that I have to deal with right now," she said, "without having to come home and feel like I can't relax around my housemates."

Unlike Donna, you may feel ready to surrender to an in-house love. Sara's idiosyncracies that once annoyed the "hell" out of you may become emdearing after a series of late night talks on the battered living room couch. Gradually you explore the subtleties of each other's psyches and then one night return to your room to explore each other's physiques. Call it love. Call it lust. What could be more convenient than having an affair with the girl or boy next-floor?

What could be more damaging to the stability of your household than such an affair? Love can afford to be blind unless your lover is also your housemate. It's very simple: In-house amours immediately exclude the rest of the house. Erica, a writer in a rural group house in Burlington, Vermont, vividly remembers how she felt when an affair started up in her house:

Sharon had always liked Darryl and lately had started speaking of him quite a lot to me—not lusting after him but just in an admiring way. One day, I came home and Sharon and Darryl were sitting on the living room couch in the dark. They weren't speaking or touching, but it seemed to me as if they had become one person and the space between them—somehow the electrons were flowing. You could have taken a pencil and drawn an outline over their heads and around them, as if they were in a huge plastic bag. You could tell that they had been touching intimately.

They just looked up and said "Hi!" very nonchalantly, but I had such a sense that I was suddenly an intruder.

What if Sharon and Darryl had been more discreet, maintaining a flippant housemate facade except in the privacy of their rooms? In group houses, however, there is no discretion as far as relations between housemates are involved. Even if Erica hadn't walked in on that telling scene on the couch, the affair between her two housemates made itself known in other ways. Darryl suddenly became very gregarious at bed-time, saying a hearty goodnight to everyone in the house. He would close his door very noisily, wait until the rest of the house was settled in their various rooms, and then sneak across creaking floors and down the stairs to Sharon's room. Someone on a midnight trip to the bathroom would inevitably see Darryl's door wide open and the light on. All his careful maneuverings were for naught. It only takes some creaking floorboards or a pencil-thin line of electrons flowing around you and your housemate/lover to set you apart, making it seem to the rest of the house as if you are claiming private turf in what were once communal areas.

Once a love relationship starts in a house, the questions remain: "Will it thrive or flounder? Will the household survive?" If your relationship thrives, that means good news for the two of you and probably bad news for the rest of the housemates who suddenly become outsiders. If the relationship flounders, then it's bad news for the whole household. Staying in the same house with someone you once felt deeply about can be tortuous for everyone. Julie, a waitress who lives in a lively Montreal group house, told us:

> It's really awkward to eat breakfast with people who
> are having problems. There was a case where a couple
> was sleeping together, and the woman was just having
> fun while the man was falling in love. All of us were
> suffering watching this the whole time. It really jeopar-
> dized the nice calm feeling of being friends because
> there was this sexual tension, and it was just dreadful.

Eventually, the man moved out and peace was restored. In Erica's house, Sharon ended up moving out, not because the affair was over but because she and Darryl wanted to stay on good terms with housemates as well as with each other. All of the housemates attended Sharon and Darryl's wedding a year later!

Moving out, though never an easy step, seems the most sensible and mature way to handle matters when the love affair proves either serious or disastrous. Betsy Neal of Roommates Preferred reports that she has seen plenty of couples who met in group houses and later married. She related the story of one man who met his true love in a group house, married her, divorced, and came back to Roommates Preferred looking for another group house.

Is there any way to prevent romantic trauma from occurring in your house so that people won't be forced to leave? There aren't any pat "how-to's" on this literally touchy topic, but you *can* do as Julie's house did after their in-house affair dissolved. At a house meeting, they addressed the problem of romances between housemates by forming a no incest policy—what Julie called a "joke rule." Since it isn't likely that you'll put "sex between housemates" on the agenda for the next house meeting, the most you can do is be aware of the risks of getting involved with a housemate, or you can take steps to make sure sexual situations won't occur such as entering a single sex house.

Alternative Views—Good Bedfellows Can Make Good Housemates

If you've found yourself scoffing at the idea of having an incest taboo between housemates, you'll be heartened to know that there are some houses that do not consider sexual attraction between housemates a liability. A few households even court it. In Ellen's house, for instance, one of the members, Jamie, shares her husband with Jim. In fact, Jamie wants to have a baby with Jim. None of the housemates feel resentful or anxious about this menage in their midst becasue they were asked at the outset if they felt comfortable with lesbian, gay, and intrahouse sexual relations. Other households, while not founded on the concept of in-house sexuality, are just more relaxed when it happens. A member of one such household, Danielle, said:

> We had a lot of musical beds. We had women sleeping
> with women—there was a time when two women in
> our house moved into a bedroom together for five days
> and came out only for scotch. We had one girl's
> boyfriend decide he was actually in love with someone
> else in the house. He used to come and visit on
> weekends, and one weekend instead of staying on the
> second floor, he stayed on the third floor. . . . Another
> time, two roommates got together and surprised
> everybody.

Another instance in which sexual attraction between housemates is not a high liability is when the housemates/lovers began their relationship prior to entering the house. These couples—whether married or unmarried—don't have as much potential for alienating housemates as couples that start in-house, and a stable couple can actually be a good influence on the rest of the housemates. Paul, a temporary worker in Washington, D.C., shared a house with a couple and three other men and women. Andy and Jean, both first year law students, provided the nucleus around which the house revolved. It was another "have your cake and eat it, too" arrangement that group living is famous for: Andy and Jean gave the house a family feeling without the prohibitive ties of a real family. In turn, living in a group house gave Andy and Jean the privacy of their own room but the option to interact with others.

Besides tempering an intense love relationship with interaction, group living offers couples: a less expensive way to live together, a chance to test their relationship before living together exclusively or marrying, and a way to share responsibilities and be less dependent on one another. What couples must watch for, however, is that they separate their roles as part of a couple and as housemates. It's very frustrating to other housemates when couples act as a bloc in house matters.

On the other hand, a couple should be attentive to their shared relationship when they enter a group house. Time and energy gets diffused by the presence of others, and lovers can easily grow apart. Couples should take time to do romantic things together away from the house, as well as making sure that lover's quarrels don't come up on the agenda for the next house meeting. As one member of duo within a group of six said, "If living with John, Robert, Mary, and Therese isn't a real test of Pat's and my relationship . . . then, hell, I don't know what is."

Children as Housemates

Like a series of Russian nesting dolls, one issue begets another. If we talk of couples flourishing within the group milieu, then what about children? While parenting in group houses is not widely practiced, it is fast becoming a practical option, especially for single parents. Imagine being able to take shifts in childcare and housework and have the rest of your time free for work or leisure. In the meantime, your conscience is at rest because your children are being cared for by adults you know and trust. In Marin County, California, known for having one of the highest divorce rates in the country, six single mothers were able to pool parenting responsibilities in just this fashion. The organizer, Polly Leach, wanted to "create an extended family . . . where everybody lends a hand and nobody was ever lonely," reported *The New York Times.*⁴ Yet, Polly was also "leery of communal living," because of the supposed lack of cleanliness and discipline. Consequently, she created a very structured household. Each parent works a minimum of three childcare shifts—morning, afternoon, or evening—a week. Each mother cooks three times a week, eighteen fewer meals than she would if she lived alone.

For parents who are turned off by the idea of sharing housing with so many adults and children, a single parent partnership makes more sense. Roommate referral services are good places to turn if you are looking for one other parent to share with. And, those who would rather not deal with anyone else's kids but their own should consider moving into houses with single men and women.

Nonparents often find that the advantages of group living with children outweigh the annoyances—the toys on the floor or Atari games on the television screen. Said Eleanor, twenty-one, fresh out of Oberlin College, "Living with kids is good for me. It gives me a better sense of reality. When living with all college students, you get a narrow perspective of what life is like." Singles also get more perspective on what having children really entails—the dirty diapers behind the happy morning hug. Tom, the man who used to live in Eleanor's room, decided he didn't want to father children after seeing firsthand what it involved. He said that he'd rather keep living in group houses with kids where he'd get all of the joys, but few of the responsibilities.

What about the children? Do children in group houses spend their wonder years being shunted from one housemate to the next, or do they grin cherubically, eat natural peanut butter, and make daisy chains to hang on the lampshades? Neither. As with every aspect of group life, children have their share of both joy and frustration.

In the late 1970s, D. Kelly Weisberg interviewed adults and children in a number of so-called "urban communes" in the Boston area. She found that children in group houses learned early to interact with *all* sorts of people and to articulate their wishes well because they had to make themselves heard in the collective clamor. The children told her they had "more" of everything —more companionship, more people to help with homework or teach them new skills, and even more birthday or Christmas presents.

On the flip side, Weisberg found that these children also have more "bosses" to contend with. She has labeled their predicament of facing many unrelated authority figures "The Cinderella Effect" and tells how one five-year-old described it, ". . . there's a lot of people that chase you around and tell you what to do."[5]

Children can also grow quite attached to some of their "inherited parents," and then must learn the pain of parting when housemates leave. Mosy, who lived all of her 2½ years in a group house with her parents and five others, is already aware of this sad fact. When her favorite housemate, Janis, moved out, mother and daughter later went to visit her, and Mosy asked, "Why do you live *here* and not with *us*?" At the same time, when Mosy and father, Simon, play "the globe game," she is able to name and point out countries as far afield as "Tan-Zan-NEEE-A" or "Oh-Stray-LA" where her globe-trotting housemates have traveled.

Practical Tips for Parents in Group Houses

For parents who have decided in principle to endorse the "more is merrier" philosophy, there are some practicalities you'll have to consider.

Childproofing. As a parent, you're probably very aware of the dangers of uncapped medicine vials and knives left on the kitchen counter, but the singles you live with won't be. Chip, a thirty-three-year-old policeman who shared with an unwed mother, her child, and four others, told how his house learned about childproofing the hard way. "When Courtney was one-and-a-half years old, she was at the stage where she was getting into everything. One day she crawled into Andrew's room and started eating some of his medicine. Luckily we were able to get her to the hospital." After that incident, they closed bottles, kept cleaning fluids on top of the fridge, covered the electrical outlets, and Chip made certain his gun was safe from Courtney. Childproofing requires constant vigilance, and parents shouldn't feel bad about reminding errant housemates since their child's safety is on the line.

You might also have to "adultproof" the house. For instance, keep stray Leggos and Barbie dolls from underfoot, and close housemate's doors when they aren't home in order to keep out curious kids.

Babysitting. One of the beauties of shared living for parents is being able to run to the store with a clear conscience, knowing your child is being watched. You can count on housemates for this informal childcare, but don't assume anything beyond that. Set up a babysitting policy from the outset. Many parents use outside sitters exclusively to avoid conflicts with housemates. Some pay their housemates to sit, and all say that the best route is to make clear to housemates that babysitting, while welcome, is not expected. Even parents who live with other parents and trade babysitting should be diligent about keeping the amounts near equal. One mother, Roseanne, who is married and currently a full-time mother, resented her single-parent housemate for treating her like a day care center. "Just because I was home, she decided I didn't have anything better to do than watch her children."

Deflecting The "Cinderella Effect." Make clear-cut decisions about who does the child-rearing and disciplining. Do the children heed just their own parents or all adult housemates? Parents who share with other parents have to deal with children's acute peripheral vision: How come John gets to stay up until 9:30, and I have to go to bed at 8:00? You can try to explain differences in decisions to children. If they accept it, fine. If not, you'll have to come up with a group standard; perhaps a 9:00 bedtime would solve the problem.

And what about punishment when a child disobeys the rules? Should non-parents feel free to discipline a noisy child? What if one parent believes in spankings now and then while another parent believes in "creative non-violence?" Parents should hold a pow-wow on the punishment problem and should be open about their expectations of housemates. Kim is the mother of a girl, five, and a boy, eight. She shares a house with all non-parents and said, "Initially, I had to keep encouraging housemates to feel free with my kids—to discipline them, ask them to be quiet, say 'no you can't come in,' or just be more assertive with them."

To avoid antagonizing children with the inevitable "do's and don'ts," give them a voice in household matters. After all, they are housemates, too. One single father decided that his son, Charlie, was great at screening out undesirables when the house interviewed prospective housemates. If someone didn't interact with Charlie, then that person wouldn't be a good housemate. It can be fun for everyone when a child's request is heard and answered, for instance, a gallon of ice cream on shopping day for spontaneous sundaes.

Saying Goodbye. While nothing can lessen the immediate pain a child feels upon saying goodbye to a departing housemate, children in group houses learn the lesson of loss at an earlier age than their peers. They soon realize that with each goodbye there also follows a hello in the form of a new housemate. However, if your children are very young, you might alleviate their confusion or hurt by taking them to visit the much-missed housemate. It will show them that while housemates leave, they aren't "all gone."

Guests and Pests

Remember when you were little, and there was always a house in the neighborhood where all the kids congregated—where you went to sleep "overnight," to play hide-and-seek, to hang out and watch "Gilligan's Island," or to turn the den into a spookhouse? Group houses are often the adult version of the childhood refuge with the worn welcome mat. A friend in a house of six people told us how she was throwing a little something into the wok, ready to settle down to a private meal with Dan Rather, and before she knew it she was preparing an elaborate Chinese dinner with her housemate Rick and three of his friends. After dinner they sat sipping coffee while she luxuriated in a newfound connection with a fellow antique dealer. Impromptu dinner parties, gatherings, and slumber parties of a sort happen often at her house and at other group houses around the country. Why? Because people who move into group houses are by nature social creatures (and those who aren't shortly become ones) and because people can afford to be social in group houses. You have much more room to put people up—friends, strangers, relatives. Not many people have that much space at their disposal, especially those who live in efficiencies in large cities.

Although there is enormous potential for the successful cross wiring of each other's friends in your group house, there is just as much potential for all the connections to explode like too many plugs in an overloaded circuit. Dinner guests now and then or friends crashing overnight on the couch may not matter much, but what happens when people overstay their welcome?

In some houses guests can never overstay their welcome. "Any stable, hospitable house will attract a psychopath or two—people who are looking for an anchor," warns Lenny, the political organizer from San Francisco. His household represents one way of treating house guests, both invited and uninvited:

One of the principles we established at the outset was one of hospitality, that we always wanted to have a guest room open. It was a reaction, in part, to the opulence of the place. We had to share the wealth. Also the core group of people who started the house

*were all world travelers. We felt that guests would end
up bringing us more—not in a material way. It was
also against our principle to be rude to a guest. Our
house was open to the community. We had crazy people too. There were a couple of people who were considered "out-patient" types who would come and camp
out in the living room.*

Lenny's household believed that the purpose of living in a group
house goes beyond fulfilling the needs of the housemates to serving
ths community—providing a place where folks can hang out. In
fact, one guest did so in the full sense of the word when he made a
habit of walking on his hands, naked, into the kitchen, genitals
gyrating, a habit that "justifiably upset the women in the house."

Brian and his housemates, all activists for world peace, go a
step further by promoting the use of their house as a forum for
political meetings and discussion:

*All of us are members of organizations—whether it's
Protestors for Women's Pentagon Action or Ultimate
Frisbee. We have meetings here. We really use this
space. Next weekend Frank is holding a meeting for
the gay Quakers here. Thirty-six people stayed in the
house over this past weekend. Usually guests will
either bring something or put money into the kitty. We
have many friends of the house. We also have some
friends who are Marines. They don't like the barracks
so they come here. We offer them a little more variety.
We're able to give them alternate opinions and
literature. For instance, we don't want the word "kill"
used in this house. And at brunch this morning, one
Marine said he was going to kill his muffin. We said,
"You don't need that, and we don't need that." We
have all kinds of people staying in this house ... all
kinds.*

There are still other houses that, although they open their doors to the public, are more selective. Teresa, the owner of a spacious Washington, D.C., townhouse with eight people and nine bedrooms, kept the extra room open for visiting performers. A playwright herself, Teresa made it known to local theatres and concert halls that she would put performers up for free. Teresa told us they had dined with an Iranian princess, ballerinas from the corps of the New York City Ballet, and a renowned dramatist.

Teresa's situation, however, is an exception. You are more likely to be entertaining your housemate's old friend George, who comes unannounced to your house while he is looking for a job and ends up staying two months, than a slender and gracious ballerina who eats only lettuce and cottage cheese. Tony's house, for instance, ended up being literally eaten out of "house and home" by a visiting friend of a friend who weighed 300 pounds and took up residence on their couch for a couple of months. Keep this incident in mind as a "worst case," and consider these guidelines for good house guestmanship:

- Agree to announce the arrival of "extended stay" guests at least a day in advance. Your house should also decide how many days constitute this. With overnight guests you can be less formal—a note on the 'fridge saying "the body on the living room couch belongs to my brother." Exceptions to this might be sudden arrivals and boyfriends/girlfriends.

- Decide how long a guest can stay without making any contribution and what that contribution should be. One household decided that after three weeks the guest has to chip in for rent and utilities. If you share food, you can work guests into your payment plan.

When you have a guest over, suggest that he or she:

- Make some kind of contribution to the house—money for groceries, food, or even a bottle of wine now and then.

- Follow the rules of the house. If your guest is a smoker and your house is a non-smoking house, for instance, suggest that your guest smoke outside or in your room with the door shut.

- Be as invisible as possible if the stay is for a number of weeks. Nothing is as irritating as waiting an hour for the bathroom, but it's twice as irritating if the shower hog isn't a housemate. Guests should also be careful not to leave their things strewn about the house.

Lovers and Other Strangers

Most guests come and go... but some guests never leave. Usually people who end up spending significant amounts of time at the house are housemates' significant "others." This is when the line between guest and live-in-lover becomes hazy. If you share food, we're assuming live-in-lovers contribute just as everyone else does, but when do you ask them to start paying rent and utilities? This is something best hashed out with all housemates at a house meeting. Special circumstances, however, should be accomodated. One of you may have a lover you don't get to see very often—someone who is in the military or away at school. When they drop in out of the blue, everyone will just have to grin and bear it. Leslie, a publicist at a publishing house in New York City, has a boyfriend who lives in Germany. When he comes to the States twice a year, he stays at her house for a six-week period. The house decided not to make him pay rent because Kurt contributes as much to the house as the others. He goes shopping, helps with the cleaning, repairs leaky faucets: In short, Kurt is a model housemate, as many houseguest/lovers are since they are trying so hard. For her part, Leslie admits that in payment for her housemates' accomodating nature, she keeps her mouth shut about things that ordinarily would annoy her.

Whether lovers become temporary housemates or not, there is a certain strain implicit in their dealings with the rest of the house that is absent with visiting firemen, group house groupies, or friends of the house. There's a tug of war between the feelings created by co-existing relationships. For instance, when you have your lover over you probably don't make much of an effort to integrate him into the household. Wherever you both are is suddenly home. You have spent so much time and agony getting acclimated to his temperament and idiosyncracies that you assume that the rest of the house will be instantly familiar with them. Then when it appears that they aren't and they get irked at poor Rodney, your allegiance to housemates will be torn as you shift to Rodney's side to unruffle his feathers and placate him.

On the other hand, live-in-lovers become easy targets for the wrath of the housemates. The unnecessary needling of lovers seems to be more common in all-female houses. One woman, Linda, suggested that this happens because women are brought up to compete for male attention, to validate their own sense of worth by having a man at their side. Three of her five housemates have boyfriends that spend time at the house. The two who don't have boyfriends made these men feel uncomfortable even though they were hardly ever there and one in particular was a model housemate. Said Linda, "It's kind of a constant reminder that they don't have boyfriends there. That's what a lot of our blow-outs are about." Always, whenever you find yourself leaking hostility towards housemates and their lovers, think about whether your feelings are related to their actions or to something gone awry in your life.

These discrepancies in perception will only be changed by awareness and conscious adjustment of those perceptions. By far the most cut-and-dried, easy-to-deal-with problem posed by extra-house affairs brought indoors is *privacy*. Extra-house lovers claim turf in a different way than in-house lovers do. With the latter it's more psychological; you *feel* like an intruder when you walk in on them talking in the kitchen because of what you know goes on between them in private. With extra-house lovers, it's all to physiological or, as one person put it, "sickening." Said Sharon, a student at Berkeley, of the romances in her house:

> *Lovers, as a unit, make others feel uncomfortable. One woman had a boyfriend, and when they were in the kitchen, you just weren't welcome. They had a way of wanting privacy in a group house. You just can't demand that. I find that a real problem myself. . . . When John came to visit, I remembered it was his birthday, and I went out and bought nice seafood. I figured Friday night at 8:30 or 9:00 the kitchen would be free, but for some reason people decided to watch television in the kitchen, which hardly every happens. So, we had to go out.*

It is unreasonable to expect that when your housemates are out they'll stay out. If you and your lover take advantage of the sudden "gift" of an empty house, group house living can turn into bedroom farce. You're rolling around on the living room rug, having left a regular Hansel and Gretel trail of undergarments behind you. Creak! Thwang! You hear the ominous banging of the screen door, and the frantic scramble for clothes begins. You feel embarassed, adolescent, and resentful, even though you know your housemate has a perfect right to walk in. The moral of that story is, "Keep it in your room with the door locked."

Making Room for Each Other While You Give Each Other Room

When you move into your group house, especially if you've lived in a dorm room, studio apartment, or an efficiency, you'll be overwhelmed by the luxury of having space to stretch out in. After you've lived there a few days, however, you realize that the space decreases in proportion to how many people are sharing it. You'll find people bumping elbows in the kitchen, people waiting anxiously in line to use the bathroom, people staking out territory in the living room, and people mysteriously congregating at the same time in the living room. Until you've lived in a group house you don't know how many hours you can spend sitting on the living room couch being thoroughly entertained. Fireplaces and television sets ordinarily give divergent housemates reason to gather; once housemates are together, the possibilities are limitless. One household had frequent discussions and debates on nuclear power; another group had a pajama party and told chain stories by the fire. Yet another household acted out Chekhov plays in their living room while one housemate videotaped the performance, and one group house played sardines during an electrical blackout and ended up trying to squeeze eight people into the bathtub. (Whoever had bathroom duty that week worked hard scrubbing out footprints.)

Just as you have cavities of loneliness or isolation that the spontaneous togetherness fills, you also have times when people crowd you, when you wish you could snap your fingers and everyone would disappear. The challenge of space sharing is to make the communal rooms in your house (living room, dining area, kitchen) into inviting gathering places and, at the same time, allow people to go about their individual business without colliding. To accomplish the first half of this task, make sure no one lets their personal clutter collect in the communal areas. Otherwise people gradually and often unconsciously stake out personal territory. It happens in student houses when someone plops their typewriter down on the dining room table, That's fine, while she's typing a paper or report, but when she goes, the typewriter should go, too. The daily newspaper can also take over a house like some furniture-swallowing monster—one section draped over the couch, one over a chair. Hey, there's the housemate you hadn't seen in weeks snoozing under the sports page with the results of the college basketball playoffs imprinted on his face. You certainly don't want to make your house into a hospital waiting room which, by its antispetic aura, says plainly "Don't be comfortable here." Without planning to, an energy-efficient household made their living room into a cozy gathering place by not using central heating during the winter. When their bedrooms felt like the inside of a refrigerator, they had no choice but to come together in the living room to warm themselves by the fire.

In most group houses, however, everyone has their own heated room. When you want that sense of life apart from your housemates, the first and most obvious dictum is: respect a closed door and close you own. Granted, you shouldn't feel like you must live in your room, but if you are a private person, expect to spend a lot of time there. For maintaining privacy, the long telephone extensions cord is as necessary as the closed door. It's nerve-racking to have to make personal phone-calls in the kitchen or hallway while everyone is stepping over your feet—too much like life in the dorms. Unintentional eavesdroppers on highly classified conversations don't enjoy themselves either. One man told us how he had to hear a housemate's distraught conversations with her boyfriend while he was commencing dinner and found himself feeling so tense he couldn't eat.

Murmurs and Booms on the Group House Decibel Scale

Noise is a bugaboo in group houses. It will make even the most resilient tempers snap—especially in student houses. Some households solve this problem by designating blocks of time as study or quiet times. Typing can be a problem because of last-minute, late-night paper stints. You can't tell someone not to type when their academic success depends on it, but you can tell them to type in the area of the house furthest away from sleeping housemates. Also, putting a pad under the typewriter helps muffle the noise.

Another souce of noise . . . shoes. Teresa, owner of a group house for eight, had to expel a housemate because she clomped up and down the wooden stairs in her wooden clogs until it drove Teresa and everyone else crazy. After Teresa told Jenny that she had to leave, Teresa found out from a mutual friend that telling Jenny not to clomp was like "telling her not to breathe." Maybe Teresa should simply have asked Jenny not to wear shoes in the house. As mentioned earlier, shoeless houses are in vogue on the West Coast. Going shoeless saves wear and tear on wooden floors, as well as healthy eardrums, and keeps grit and grime outside where it belongs (important in major cities!).

Shoes, typewriters, telephone talk, and concurrent conversations are gentle murmurs on the group house decibel scale compared to the booming vibrations of that coveted item, the stereo. The average American group house, if surveyed, would probably boast three stereos under each roof. It's a lucky thing, too, since you'll live with people at both ends of the musical spectrum—Khatchaturian to Kiss. Most groups admit that volume is more of a problem than differing musical tastes. One house had a rule that you don't turn the stereo up late at night unless you can get everyone else to party with you. Better still, set specific times after which cranking the stereo up becomes "illegal." You could even agree on a volume level not to be surpassed except at house parties. Practice the words, "turn it down, please," while being prepared to heed those words. You'll find that some people need a dose of high-volume music to keep them charged through the day. Ann, an education student at a community college in Baltimore, related that she was constantly awakened by extremely loud rock 'n'roll music at a time much earlier than she wanted to get up (6:00 a.m.). Finally, she knocked on Tom's door (the culprit) and saw him, hair slicked back from his morning shower, sitting tautly on the edge of the bed, shaking his head to the music. "I felt afraid to interrupt by asking him to turn the volume down." The problem was solved when Tom's housemates, spurred by Ann, bought him headphones for his birthday. Politeness and courtesy will take you so far, but headphones, as a member of one quadrophonic house claims, are "God's gift to group houses."

Keeping Your House from "Going Down the Tube"

The television set is a possible drawing card for living room gatherings, but once housemates surround the set, they may realize that three, four, or more is not "company" during prime time. When there's one television set for more than one viewer the crucial question becomes, Who will we share the living room with, the Family Feud team, Luke from General Hospital, or the San Diego Chargers?

"We had terrible television fights," confesses Barry, a carpenter in an Oakland, California, household. "Pam and I would be saying we wanted to watch something, David immediately heard us and dashed out right away to the T.V. He claimed he was there first and went and watched what he wanted, but we always had the first intention to watch something." Are you going to watch "Masterpiece Theatre" or the NFL playoffs? In Barry's house the strongest will won, and David had the strongest will. He also owned the television set, yet he kept it downstairs for everyone to use. Said Barry, "If you do keep your T.V. in your room, it's a little obnoxious, but at least it defines your territory. Everyone knows it's your T.V., and they can ask permission if they want to use it."

What wins out? Intent, will, or ownership rights? Your household will have to decide. If tastes consistently don't coincide but program times do, you should consider buying another "house television." Many groups we talked to didn't think twice about having two refrigerators and seven stereos, yet the idea of having two television sets seemed gauche—too "nuclear family-ish." Having two tellys solves problems in a family so the kids can watch the late-night horror movie while Mom and Dad watch Johnny Carson in their bedroom. Why couldn't putting up a few bucks for a second-hand black and white T.V. end video wars in your house? This solution is especially effective if you are living with a television addict, someone who has learned the fine art of letting the fork find his mouth when he eats dinner with his eyes glued to the screen. As with everything in group house life, a little consideration on everyone's part, the addicted and the afflicted, will do a lot to improve a difficult situation.

If matters have deteriorated so that the once reasonable adults in your house suddenly become stubborn children staunchly defending their video rights, then negotiations will have to continue on that level. In other words, barter: "David, if you let me watch this show tonight, I'll clean your dirty dishes tomorrow."

Pooling Your Possessions: Mine? Yours? or Ours?

- If you want to use it and it doesn't belong to you, get permission.
- If you borrow it, return it.
- If you use it, take care of it.
- If you don't know how to operate it, leave it alone.
- If you break it, repair it.
- If you can't fix it, get someone who can.

The above maxims, excerpted from Betsy Neal's "Roommates' Golden Rules," should be committed to each housemate's memory if you want to keep "possession anxiety" down in your house. Possession anxiety occurs when you unpack your wares—from saucepan to stereo—to add to the communal stock. You shiver with fear at the thought of your plates getting bunged in the dishwasher when they should be sponged delicately by hand. You wince as you watch a housemate pick the dust off your stereo's needle with his fingertips.

Whether Betsy's rules are heeded or not, when you contribute items to the house you should *accept the fact that they will be used by others and that, in the course of being used, they may be damaged or destroyed.* It's not that group houses are half-way houses for the careless; they are full of human beings and human beings (especially children) have accidents. Don't donate the china you inherited from Grandma Leticia if you know your heart will break when it does.

What about less sentimental, more essential, items that you want to share but that need proper use and care—a teflon pan, wok, stereo, enamel dish, or toaster oven? When you share these things, don't feel shy about telling people exactly how they should be used. Likewise, when a housemate tells you not to put her enamel soup bowls in the dishwasher, respect that. Perry, a thirty-three-year-old who admits that he's more finicky than the younger people he shares a townhouse with, said that besides handling with care, it's important to show concern when you forget:

> *I've got a couple of teflon pans that have gotten scratched because people have used metal. O.K., I've done that too, on occasion. I think I responded with a little bit of concern for the fact that I'd done that. Here the people treat the matter a bit more cavalierly, saying, "that's the price you pay for having stuff." Well, they can say that when they don't have any kitchen equipment . . . I just got a Cuisinart and I finally told people not to use it because I don't want that issue to come up.*

Ideally, you shouldn't have to put either verbal or written labels on your things—"Perry's Cuisinart, don't touch." When you and five others share the possessions you've acquired separately, it is a delight to find you suddenly have "all the conveniences of home" when you aren't bringing home enough cash to support one blender. Some group houses resemble the kitchen appliance section of Sears and Roebuck with blenders, food processors, pasta machines, and even K-Tel salad whirlers. One of the biggest advantages of group living, in fact, is the sudden wealth you acquire when you share the things you each have, making a whole far greater than the sum of its parts.

How to Keep Furniture and Other Essential Items From Disappearing When Housemates Do.

What does a group do when a housemate departs taking his T.V. and toaster oven with him, and his replacement brings nothing but a mattress and a blanket? Just as your house can suddenly inherit a sleep sofa and dining room table, it can, suddenly, be stripped bare of draperies, plates, and chairs. You may also be faced with the dilemma of housemates who leave their things in the house but come back later to retrieve them. Tony, member of a six-person, two-dog household, told how a former housemate calls periodically and threatens to take back the washing machine he left there a year ago. When this man first called up there was a moment of panic as Tony considered the loss of the house's chief convenience. Since this fellow never followed through, the housemates wash their clothes in peace!

Unfortunately, most houses don't plan for the gain and loss of house property either small or large. But you can decide how to acquire items without leaving your house bare when housemates move out. First, what *not* to do: Don't use the interview process as a way to cull washing machines or whatever else your house fancies. Remember, appliances and furniture don't necessarily come with good housemates.

The most sensible way to obtain small essentials like brooms, glasses, and pots is to pay for them out of the same household fund that buys your toilet tissue and lightbulbs. After all, it's unlikely that a housemate will be sore when she leaves without being reimbursed for her 59ᶜ share in the squeegee mop. You should be more cautious about splitting the cost of furniture and other expensive things since you have to consider the following variables: the permanence of your household, its members' standard of living, and their different decorating taste.

When Sally and five friends at the University of Massachusetts at Amherst set up housekeeping together during their second year of school, they didn't have a stitch of furniture except a pink formica kitchen dinette table. Though all were on student incomes, they managed to pool enough money to buy a coffee table, couch, an oak table with chairs, and bookshelves at local flea markets and garage sales. When two members of the house moved out the following year, their replacements paid the former housemates for a share of the furniture, minus the cost of wear and tear. At the end of the fourth year, they drew lots and everyone claimed a piece to keep. This arrangement works well if you have a core group of people who know each other and plan to live in a house for a few years. Other groups with ample incomes yet barren rooms should consider renting furniture, adding the cost to their rent. And households with even more cash on hand might prefer to have members purchase items individually instead of collectively. A three-family household (three couples and two children) in Philadelphia collected their furniture in this manner; one family bought a couch, another family bought a dining room table and chairs, while the third family bought coffee tables, lamps and an easy chair. The cost of their separate purchases equaled out more or less, and they liked the idea of owning pieces separately just in case the household broke up. Then, there are the creative group houses whose members make their own furniture. A "home made" group house collection would include some of the following items:

- Bookshelves made of planks and cinder blocks,
- Tables made from telephone-wire spools, tree trunks, or doors on sawhorses,
- A couch fashioned from an old twin bed with a fitted cover and colorful cushions,

- A kitchen storage area erected from plastic milk crates,
- Chairs made out of wooden crates,
- Wallhangings that were once bedspreads,
- Curtains that were once sheets,
- Lots of plants in wicker hampers to hide bare spots.

Beware of Free Loaders

In addition to pitching in to purchase furniture, you and your housemates may want to go in together on other costly but necessary items—a second refrigerator, a washing machine and dryer, or a newspaper subscription. Some people who can't even swing subscribing to *The New York Times* on their own end up being able to peruse it along with a host of magazines when they enter a group house. Unfortunately, a fraction of these people enjoy the new privileges of group living without pitching in their portion of the dough. Enter the freeloader.

The term "freeloader" may have been coined in a group house. Perhaps one day, a household was discussing their desire to buy a washer and dryer rather than walk five blocks to the local laundromat, but one housemate stubbornly refused to go in with the others. Once the Maytag was installed, however, this housemate ended up getting a "free load" by tiptoeing down the basement steps when everyone else was asleep and doing three loads of wash. In any group house, a freeloader is like a weight chained to everyone's feet dragging the house spirit—not to mention the house budget—down. Once you catch a freeloader in the act, the issue is clear-cut: it's pay up or get out. If someone becomes particularly ornery you could threaten to take their share out of the security deposit. The best tack is to stop freeloading before it starts by having consensus on large purchases. Sometimes a housemate will be earnestly unsure of whether he'll use the item in question. Suggest a trial period in which he and the rest of the house can gauge his use of Home Box Office, *Time* magazine, or the new trash compacter. After the trial period is up you can all meet to decide if he should pay up. Remember, though, that everyone is going to end up using different things, different amounts of time. Once again, it is important to believe that "it will all even out in the end."

Decorating by Committee

Barry's living room boasts a red shag rug, a floral-patterned divan, an impressive mahogany bookcase, three milk crates housing records, and a wooden torso on wheels (one of his housemate's attempts at art). His living room, however odd, is decorated in the prevailing group house decor: Early Eclectic. You'll find groups that have mini flea-markets in their living rooms. There are well-to-do group dwellers whose living and dining rooms look like the auction hall of Sotheby Parke Bernet. And, horror of horrors, you'll come across houses where "mother's best sofa" co-exists with discount store throw pillows.

A well-coordinated living room in a group house, although rare, is not impossible to achieve. You may enjoy the divine accident of shared tastes. More realistically, one housemate with the inspiration and inclination will oversee the purchasing and decorating. In a household of seven women, Charlotte, the only non-student at the time, enjoyed spending her free time collecting things to spruce up the house. She refinished an old wooden hat rack, found a frame for a housemate's Maxfield Parrish print, reupholstered a chair, and painted the walls light blue. Charlotte also spent household money for all of these projects on the condition that she solicited each housemate's approval first.

However, when members dip into their own pockets or into boxes of castoff knick-knacks from their parent's house, don't expect to get first refusal rights on the house decor. Most group houses take the tasteful meets tacky trauma in stride. "Something we absolutely, unequivocally do not agree upon is artwork and furniture arranging," said Don in a late night bull session around his house's dining room table (which, by the way, had been moved three times in the course of a month). "All of us have our own unique preferences that are never going to change. It's also kind of funny when all of the sudden you realize that somebody hates a picture that's been up all year—like that one over the fireplace that looks like it belongs in a mobile home." "Hey, wait a minute," Steve, the painting's owner, butts in. "That's my favorite painting." And so it goes.

When it's not the decor but the decorum you take issue with, you may have a bone to pick. . . or rather, a poster to peel. This is exactly what one concerned parent did to her housemate's pornographic foldouts.

Furry Housemates

"All things being equal," said one unwilling keeper of his housemate's cat, "don't have a pet in a group house." But all things are never equal, and people will continue to adopt un-housebroken pups, pernickety cats, and even svelte boa constrictors into their household. If you are adamantly opposed or allergic to furry housemates, you have probably made good use of the interview process and screened for a pet-less living situation. This section is for those of you who, out of choice or accident, end up living with pets.

When you want to own a pet and live in a group house, you should seriously consider the following points:

- Housebreaking—will you have time to adequately housetrain your dog, cat, or monkey? This means spending time during the day and night until your pet is housebroken. Once housebroken, are you prepared, in the case of a cat, to maintain a clean litterbox in a place inoffensive to housemates? One woman describes not being able to eat her dinner without gagging because of the litter box's proximity to the kitchen table. Are you prepared to clean up an occasional mess your pet makes in someone's room? Will you replace any items your pet destroys or soils?

- Are you prepared to feed your pet regularly and make plans so it isn't fed five times a day by housemates who have been conned by the animal?

- Are you willing to spend money on your pet's care and upkeep (veterinary shots, battle wounds, etc.)? Have you made plans to get your puppy or kitten spayed or neutered?

- Is there room enough in your house for a pet? Will you keep it outside or inside? If inside, will the pet have the run of the house? Will people be home enough to let your pet in and out?

- If you have a pet that needs to be walked twice a day, will you be able to do that consistently? If you can't do it sometimes, will one of your housemates be *happy* to?

- Will you take responsibility for keeping your pet out of the neighbor's yard? Group house relations with neighbors can be fragile enough without your dog bounding over and eating their tulips.

If a pet owner is conscientious with respect to all of these considerations, then it's possible for you to have a very smoothly running household despite barks, dog hair, chirping, meowing, and all. But if the owner is not responsible, watch out, for housemates will spar like cats and dogs. Unlike a sink full of dirty dishes, a pet can't be ignored for days on end. If the owner or caretaker doesn't feed it, some other sympathetic housemate will, but the resentment will build up from having an unwelcome new chore.

The real housebreaker is housebreaking. It is a simple law of science: what goes in must come out but preferably not in someone's closet, behind the couch, or in a basket of fresh laundry. Ann, a graduate student at the University of Pennsylvania, refers to her experience in a group house as "the year I had my nice rug." She had to practically live in her room during a steamy Phildelphia summer since a housemate's dog had a penchant for urinating on her antique hook rug. Jamie, who lived in a Cleveland group house with one other man, a woman, and her dog, related:

> *The biggest problem in our house was that one person had a dog, and the dog was a puppy that she was try-ing to train. And she felt like the dog belonged to all of us, but we thought the dog belonged to her. We also thought she should clean up after the dog, that that wasn't part of the housework. The dog belonged to her, and the dog droppings belonged to her.*

Though the issue of housebreaking is all to evident in Jamie's house, the real issue is ownership. If it becomes increasingly clear that no one is taking proper care of the pet, find another home for it where someone will. Not only is it inhumane to the housemates to bring home a pet when everyone and no one claims responsibility, but it is very inhumane to the animal. A case in point is Janis's household, an extremely diverse group of seven, which faced the "to neuter or not to neuter" question. In a "well I've been through everything" voice typical of group house veterans, Janis said:

> *When the cat started to mature, there was the problem of whether to get him fixed. He was howling and dart-ing around with this mad energy. Ben, the owner, wanted to get him fixed but he couldn't afford to at*

*that time. Another member, Wendy, was a Catholic,
and so she didn't like the idea of it. Ted, the hippy,
wanted to let the cat outside to follow his natural in-
stincts. Bob, who was a difficult person anyway, said,
"How'd you like to get your balls cut off?" I said,
"Please, just do something soon since he's beginning to
make a mess." And Don, who was fed up with the
whole thing, threatened to take matters into his own
hands, literally. Finally, Ben borrowed some money
and had it done, but the cat had already matured so he
was uncomfortable and unhappy afterwards, and he
still howls on the occasional romantic night since his
voice has already changed.*

At least in Janis's house they could all talk openly about the
cat and the problems it caused. That's difficult to do when the pet's
owner identifies emotionally with it. Pets sometimes serve as emotional outlets for their owners—substitute lovers, children,
anything but what they really are. It can create antagonism when a
housemate is more congenial to his dog than to the other
housemates. If you recognize yourself here, you should make a concerted effort to separate yourself from your pet when housemates
lodge a pet-related complaint. Also, when you notice yourself
becoming too defensive with respect to your cat, dog, or gerbil,
your attitude could be a sign for you to make more of an effort to
socialize with your housemates or perhaps find yourself a situation
where your needs will be filled by other people and not by the pet.
Those living with an overprotective pet owner must take care too.
Phrase your remarks concerning the pet in ways that will be
helpful and not hurtful. For example, don't say, "that cat of yours is
stinking up the whole house," but "could you empty the litter box
more often?"

Of course, if you all are avowed pet lovers, the issues we've
just discussed may not even surface in your house. Tony, a member
of one such "animal house," had enough affection for his two furry

housemates that he was able to overlook incidents that might have driven someone else out:

> *Cory is Bill's dog, and Bunny is Barb's dog. Bunny barks a lot at everything . . . she's a stray with emotional problems. I enjoy playing with both dogs. Cory is very friendly and chews on things . . . chewed on one of my wool caps. I just laughed. I can afford to buy another one. She also chewed on some blankets. Bob's offered to reimburse people for the ruined things, though.*

Smokers . . . Non-Smokers . . . and Anti-Smokers

What could be more annoying than to have your cigarette snuffed out by a vigilant anti-smoker in the privacy of your own home? On the other hand, what could be more annoying than to inadvertently inhale the noxious fumes from a housemate's cigarette while you're trying to relax in the living room? If cigarette smoking is of concern to you—whether you're for or against—it makes the most sense to screen for your preference while advertising for housemates or during the interview. Honesty on both sides is absolutely necessary or you may end up in this type of unfortunate situation: Highly allergic to cigarette smoke, Elizabeth made a point of asking prospective housemates whether they smoked. She and her present housemate, Lori, eventually chose Rebecca—a vivacious law student who, besides being friendly, admitted to being a non-smoker. Come exam time, however, Rebecca was lighting up; Elizabeth's allergies were flaring up; and the household seemed to be breaking up as Lori took Elizabeth's side in the great cigarette battle. They spent a miserable three weeks during which Rebecca smoked furiously in her bedroom, and Elizabeth in the adjacent room had to keep her heating vent closed to keep the smoke from seeping in. Finally, Elizabeth and Lori asked Rebecca to leave after her exams, an additional stress she could've avoided at the outset by admitting to being an under-pressure smoker. In some instances, a houseful of smokers will also find a "non-smoker" objectionable. One such person moved into a friend's house and ended up bumming cigarettes from everyone in the house and *never* buying his own. So, whether you smoke one cigarette a month, a pack a day, or none at all, admit to it during the interview.

Some smokers join anti-smoking households (in which housemates are either allergic to cigarette smoke or against it on principle) and even live happily ever after. How? By vowing to give up smoking on moving day. For instance, Molly's desire to live in her friend Eva's group house and her desire to stop smoking were fulfilled simultaneously when she was accepted into the house. The household, dominated by anti-smokers, had known Molly through Eva and liked her, but they accepted her only on the condition that she wouldn't smoke in the house. Since she moved in six months ago, she's quit smoking except for an occasional cigarette at the restaurant where she works, plus she loves her living situation and her housemates love her. A caution: if you are allergic to cigarette smoke and considering living with someone like Molly, it's better to know and trust the person. You'll risk being physically uncomfortable if you take a stranger on his word and he doesn't follow through and kick the habit.

While it's usually disastrous for anti-smokers and smokers to team up, it is possible and very common for non-smokers and smokers to live peaceably together. Non-smokers come in widely varying degrees of tolerance to cigarette smoke. Some people don't object at all to being surrounded by a haze of smoke while others find smoking distasteful only if it is in their presence. When those in the latter category share housing with smokers, some smoking precedents should be established. Certain areas or rooms can be designated as "smoking rooms" for instance, or smokers can only light up when not in the company of those who object.

While there are things smokers can do to make life more pleasant for their non-smoking housemates, there is little either can do to prohibit smoking friends who come over. Tom, the most fervent anti-smoker in Molly's household, tried to keep people from smoking at their big Halloween party by not leaving a single ashtray out for guests. As the evening wore on, the die-hard smokers lit up anyway and were forced to flick their ashes onto the rug, the floors, and into trash baskets full of paper—a messy and potentially dangerous situation. At their next party, this time for Christmas, he made a "Please Do Not Smoke" sign and posted it in the hallway and scattered ashtrays everywhere. Fewer people smoked, and the house was in better shape the next morning.

Sign on The Dotted Line: Group Housing and the Law

Group house members are more than just housemates. They are also tenants, homeowners, neighbors, owners of cameras and stereos, and most likely, working people concerned about their financial futures.

Remember, you can do things that other people do—buy a house and insurance, be a member of a community—and still live in a group house. This chapter will provide tips and details about the special problems groups face on a number of legal and financial fronts, from zoning to insurance.

Zoning: Are We Breaking the Law?

"When I got a complaint a few weeks ago from someone about a commune in their neighborhood, I had to chuckle," a District of Columbia zoning official told us. "It had been so long."

Several years ago the complaints were more frequent. "We'd check them out," the official said, "but as far as the zoning regulations go they were okay."

Those neighbors may have had good reasons to gripe, but what they learned about the zoning laws gave them no satisfaction. For in Washington, D.C., provided they share all facilities and truly live as a "family," six unrelated adults may live together in a single-family house. So why the complaints? The zoning official continued:

That many adults in one house can cause problems. The extra cars make parking spaces harder to find, and the extra foot traffic, with all the different schedules and everybody's friends coming and going, can be noticeable. It can be annoying, and people start to fear that the neighborhood will change and become less desirable. But, unless the people are living independently in a boarding house sort of arrangement, it's not against the law.

The complaints have slacked off. People have educated themselves to accepting the arrangements, and different people are living that way. We used to get complaints about "hippies." Now young professionals are sharing houses.

While the zoning laws in the District of Columbia aren't an obstacle to group living, the same is not true everywhere. It's wise to check with the zoning commission of your local government just to be aware of what the law is, even if you don't intend to have it rule your actions. Chances are your arrangement doesn't violate the zoning laws—most municipalities permit five unrelated people to live together as a family. And even if your group surpasses the legal limit, you probably won't encounter opposition if you don't rankle your neighbors.

Neighborhood opposition to group houses is exactly what developed several years ago in Berkeley, California. In 1978, complaints by neighbors that certain group houses were congesting the streets with extra cars eventually led to a demonstration by group houses.

What started the hubbub was a proposal considered by the Berkeley City Council that would have required group houses with more than four members to furnish a parking space off the street for each additional member of their households. Hundreds of group house residents appeared at the council meeting that considered the proposal, and for three hours, dozens of speakers attacked the proposal, protesting that the measure discriminated against non-traditional, "intentional" families.

The council defeated the parking proposal, but before the meeting ended, the debate was transformed into a larger one. The question became whether or not "intentional" families should be subject to any size limitation at all. The final result was an interesting but ambiguous one—the council instructed the city staff to come up with a more "flexible" definition of household size that would take into consideration the increased incidence of non-traditional arrangements.

Although the results were inconclusive, the Berkeley group houses, as reported in the *San Francisco Chronicle," ...* showed themselves as a mobilized political force capable of throwing back what they considered an attack on their lifestyle."[6]

The Berkeley experience shows that collective action is one way to counter community opposition. But if you can avoid the wrath of your neighbors, it's unlikely that you'll be challenged on zoning grounds, even if your household does exceed the legal size. This is so because zoning laws, rather than being ends in themselves, are more a means to the end of preserving a certain character in a neighborhood. In most cases, group houses can enhance, rather than detract from, that character. Imagine two hypothetical situations. Which course would you prefer your neighborhood to take?

Scenario One. In an old neighborhood made up of six-bedroom houses, an old zoning law defines a "family" as a married couple and as many people related to them by blood as they care to fit under their roof. After all, that's who lived in these houses in the good old days—Mom, Dad, the kids, and maybe grandmother. But there's a problem. Grandmother's dead, Mom and Dad are about to become grandparents, and the kids all have condominiums in Chicago. Dad's retired and wants to move to Arizona. But no one wants, or can afford, a house that size.

Scenario Two. Mom and Dad move to Arizona but less restrictive zoning laws permit them to rent what might have been a white elephant to a group of young people just starting their careers. They start a vegetable garden, organize a paper drive in the neighborhood, and become accepted members of the community.

On the other hand, zoning may never become an issue. Listen to Ted:

> *I shared a house with six other people on one of Washington's main streets. We never knew our neighbors; in fact, the house to the right of ours was abandoned. The whole area was undergoing transition to "gentrification." I doubt anyone knew or cared that we were violating the zoning laws.*

On balance, however, it's probably better to have neighbors and get along with them. But what does being a good neighbor involve?

How to Win Over and Influence Your Neighbors

In a neighborhood where group houses are common and have been around for a number of years, there will be few problems. But in a more staid neighborhood of traditional families who have no experience with group houses as neighbors, the problem is more acute. The basic rule for being a good neighbor in this situation, which may be anathema to the non-conformists among you, is *don't make waves.* In superficial matters at least, try to uphold the standards that you notice on your street. You may feel some missionary zeal, you may want to educate your neighbors to the viability and acceptability of group living, but do it slowly.

Since appearances are usually the stuff of initial impression, that's a good place to start. In Berkeley, apparently, the proliferation of cars around group houses became a sore point for neighbors. An excess of cars can be irritating in two ways. First, it is jarring simply because it's different and a constant reminder of a new, unknown quantity in the neighborhood. More important, in an in-town neighborhood it simply makes parking spaces a lot more scarce. So if yours is a four- or five-car "family," take that into account when you look for a house. Give weight to a house with a garage or driveway, or to a neighborhood where there doesn't appear to be a serious shortage of parking places on the street.

Another solution is to do what Greg's house did in Los Angeles. "For parking," Greg said, "we'd have a rotation system. We could only comfortably fit three cars without causing a fire access problem. A person would have their week when they'd park their car at the bottom of the hill and walk up."

In a suburban neighborhood, it's important to keep your yard neat. "I hate gardening and have a brown thumb," said Jim, who lives in a suburban group house in Euclid, Ohio, outside of Cleveland. "So we do a minimal amount of lawn care. We pick up the broken twigs and mow the lawn."

The more you do on this front, the better. Jenny shares a house with two men and another woman. She and one of the men became interested in growing flowers and vegetables after moving into a suburban house in mid-winter:

> *We grew tomatoes, lettuce, and carrots that first year.*
> *The coldness we felt from our neighbors began to*
> *thaw when they saw our tomato vines. We'd moved*
> *right into the midst of an ongoing competition to see*
> *who could grow the biggest, healthiest tomatoes. Since*
> *we were newcomers, people didn't seem to mind let-*
> *ting us in on our secrets. We made a lot of new friends*
> *that way, and the added benefit was that people*
> *started to take our house for granted as they got to*
> *know us.*

Other groups have taken a more direct approach to gaining the confidence of their neighbors. "My group moved into a suburb with a bad burglary problem," Michael told us. "Our neighbors didn't know what to make of us, but when I joined the 'Neighborhood Watch' and spent one evening a month patrolling the streets in a car, our neighbors started to respect us."

Noise is another problem that occasionally comes between group houses and their neighbors. Remember the wise man who said "Headphones are God's gift to group houses." Not only do they protect one house member from the tastes or exuberance of another housemate, but they protect the entire neighborhood from them, too. The disco at 3:00 a.m. may not be your next door neighbor's idea of a good time.

Impressing Potential Landlords and Getting Along with the One You've Got

As important as it is to get along with your neighbors, a more important relationship if you're a renter is with your landlord. Your landlord can make your life miserable. Everyone had a horror story involving a landlord, but it needn't be so. When you're shopping for a house, you're also shopping for a landlord. Look him or her over carefully, and remember that he's looking you over, too. If you and your group are shopping for a house, here are a few tips on impressing a potential landlord:

- Ask for a long lease.
- If you've assembled a group but are looking for a house, put together a group resume.
- If you have a separate house bank account under the names of two or more members of the house, tell the landlord.
- Tailor your lease to take into account several co-equal tenants.
- Don't get distressed about the security deposit, but inventory the property it covers.
- If any member of your group is especially interested in honing up on home repair skills, mention that to your prospective landlord.

A long lease shows your landlord that you are settled and serious. It also relieves him from the headache of searching for new tenants. Hunting for a house is no fun, neither is hunting for a tenant.

The group resume doesn't have to be as elaborate as a job resume, but should include your names, ages, occupations, and salaries. Go one step further, and do the work for him—add up your salaries, and put the grand total at the bottom. You may not think you are very well paid (Who does?), but multiply your annual salary by three or four or five. Your "family" income probably puts you among the nation's top earners. Your landlord will respect that. Educational backgrounds and landlord references, if available, might also be added. Be honest. "Our references were really thoroughly checked," said Lisa about her first encounter with her current landlord in Miami. "She called our employers and our former landlord."

A group bank account shows a landlord that you are businesslike and organized in your finances. He'll also be glad not to have to deal with more than one rent check each month.

One property manager told us he insists on a group lease and has all the housemates sign it. The tenants are "jointly and severally liable" for the rent—that means if one tenant skips town, the remaining tenants are liable for his or her share. With this sort of lease, you have an added incentive for selecting stable and financially responsible housemates.

Property managers and landlords who have dealt with group houses recognize that turnover is inevitable. Many like to reserve the right to review new house members and to include them in the lease. They accomplish this by means of an addendum to the lease, which states simply that A has replaced B in the house and agrees to be subject to all the terms of the lease. A and the landlord then sign the addendum. But after a time, landlord approval often becomes little more than a rubber stamp. After they've selected a new housemate in Paul's house in Baltimore, the landlords require that "they meet the person, for formality's sake and to make sure he or she is a real human being—a respectable human being."

If the tenants are young and have not established credit, the landlord might request a security deposit equal to two months' rent. Older tenants, especially professionals with credit cards, should only expect to put down one month's rent.

A security deposit protects the landlord from default of rent payment and from any damage the tenant inflicts on the property. In the security deposit transaction, an essential procedure for protecting the *tenant* from an unscrupulous landlord is putting together a physical inventory of the property. Tour the house with the landlord, write down any defects you notice, and have both parties sign it. That way, the landlord cannot claim that the damage was inflicted during your tenancy. You'll also avoid a potentially divisive situation, one that can separate housemate from housemate, as well as landlord from tenant. That's what happened to Phil:

> *I was close to our landlord, and at the end of the year, he came in and gave us an inspection after everything was out of the house to kind of assess damage. He found lots of problems. He found things, though, that we didn't have anything to do with. Linda followed him around and had a big screaming battle with him. I heard it and couldn't believe she was doing that. I was afraid of losing our deposit. After Mr. C left, I had a big screaming battle with Linda. I mean why couldn't she have said calmly, "Mr. C, we don't remember that window ever being there, are you sure?" Instead of, "That goddam window was never there!" So as you can guess, Linda and I did not part as friends.*

If your landlord is interested in improving the value of his property, he may jump at the prospect of gaining skilled tenants who are willing to work on his house. It's not uncommon to make an arrangement where the landlord provides or pays for all material, and the tenant contributes labor. Fair enough. The landlord ends up with a more attractive, valuable, and desirable property, and the tenants sharpen their handyman skills and—for the duration of their tenancy—have a nicer place to live.

Paying attention to these considerations will help prevent the special circumstances of group living from creating problems between you and your landlord. Broach the questions when you have your first interview with a prospective landlord, or if you meet with him to renegotiate your lease. He'll respect your straightforward approach. If he doesn't, and prefers not to face the issues, you probably don't want to live in his house. Eventually, you'll find a landlord like this one who had faced these problems: He said, "Groups scare the hell out of a lot of people, but they don't bother us."

Stop Making Your Landlord Rich: Buy Your Group House

After you have lived in a group house for awhile and have decided that you like living this way, it will probably dawn on you that the rent check you send off each month is making no one rich but your landlord. When this thought crosses your mind, it's time to think about buying a house with your housemates.

A house as an investment isn't the only goal of cooperative house buyers. Divorced parents, for example, may find others in their situation with whom they can recreate a caring home environment. But don't ignore the financial rewards; the advantages of home ownership are well known. Not only are you preserving the money you earn in the form of a tangible asset, but you are gaining an immediate tax break as you deduct property taxes and the interest on your mortgage. To these financial advantages, add the intangible pride of ownership, and you have a move you'll seriously want to consider.

Do your considering carefully. Buying a house is a serious step for anyone, but buying in tandem with others presents added complications. Everyone who buys a house has to apply for a mortgage loan and deal with real estate agents and lawyers. Co-op buyers have to do all of this plus devise an agreement among themselves to

LANDLORD-TENANT PRIMER—A FEW BASIC PRINCIPLES OF LANDLORD-TENANT LAW

Eviction

Your landlord can evict you, but he must give you reasonable notice. In many jurisdictions, reasonable notice is equal to the length of time between rent payments.

Leases—Types

Tenancy for years: A written agreement in which both the starting date and ending date of the lease are specified.

Tenancy at will: An oral lease for an unspecified term. Usually rent is paid monthly, and a month's notice is required for eviction.

Tenancy at sufferance: A situation in which the tenant stays on the premises after a tenancy for years or other lease has expired. If the tenant pays rent and the landlord accepts it, the lease becomes a tenancy at will.

Repairs

Unless the lease specifies otherwise, a landlord in most states has no obligation to make repairs. In the vast majority of cases, however, landlords do repair for two reasons: to preserve the value of their property and to maintain good relations with their rent-paying, income-generating tenants.

Security Deposits

Some states offer extra protection to the tenant in this often troublesome area of landlord-tenant relations. In Massachusetts, for example, the landlord must pay interest on the security deposits held more than one year. If he fails to return the deposit, he may have to pay double damages.

Tenants' Rights

Many jurisdictions have enacted laws offering special protections for tenants. In some states, a landlord who threatens a tenant who is active in a tenants' union may be liable for damages. In others, leases in which landlords reserve the right to evict without notice are illegal. Check your state law for other specific tenant protections.

clarify how they will share their asset. Every expert will tell you that the worst thing you can do is buy property with others on the basis of a casual understanding.

As the recession in the housing industry deepens, experience with purchases by two or more people is growing. Condominium design has been influenced by the trend—now so-called "mingles" are purchasing condominiums that contain two master bedrooms.

Another aspect of the old practices that has been altered to accomodate a new trend is the mortgage. As one real estate expert at a Boston bank put it, "It's unusual today to have one person come in whose income can support a mortgage." Although each prospective co-owner must fill out a separate loan application and each is subject to a separate credit evaluation, each need not have a salary that will independently support the loan. The combined income will be considered. Even if one applicant has never had a credit card, it maybe possible to get a loan if a parent or older brother or sister is willing to co-sign the note. The most frequent response from savings and loans about lending to groups? "No problem."

Problems may arise, however, in the process of agreeing on how ownership of the house will be shared. "I've had a number of people approach me wanting to buy and live cooperatively," said one realtor. "But when they hear the details, ninety percent of them are scared off." We hope that won't happen to you. It will be a complicated process, but we think that if you consider the following questions, your difficulties will be eased.

How will you take title to the property?

There are a number of different forms of co-ownership, but two basic arrangements are used most frequently: joint tenancy and tenancy in common.

Joint tenants share the use of all property owned together, but do not own delineated, individual shares of the property. The repercussions of this form of ownership become stark of one owner dies.

As a joint tenant, you can leave your share of the property to whomever you want in your will, but they'll never get it. When you die, the surviving owner or owners get all the property you owned jointly with them.

As tenants in common, you and your co-owners not only share the use of your common property, but also own equal shares of the property. If you die, your share passes to your heirs.

As you learn the difference between joint tenancy and tenancy in common, you'll see that the form you choose depends a great deal on the ideological and philosophical content of your relationship with your co-owners. Joint tenants are likely to be less interested in purchasing property as an investment and more interested in the cooperative living arrangement as an end in itself. Married couples often choose this form of ownership. Tenants in common, on the other hand, are casting one eye toward the future. In other words, they probably don't intend to live on the jointly owned property forever, or they have heirs they want to leave assets to. Judy, a divorced mother of two teen-age children, entered into a tenancy in common when she bought a house with Martha. "If I died," Judy said, "I wanted to be sure the kids got a share of the house. We decided in advance that if that happened Martha would buy out their share so they would have money for college."

Will you own equal shares of the property?

An advantage to cooperative purchasing is that it allows people of different income levels to band together and enjoy the benefits of house ownership. Three individuals, for example, could own two 40 percent shares and one 20 percent share of a house. The hitch is that the perfect equality is lost in this arrangement, and the owners wilth larger shares might feel they deserve more votes in house decisions. Ken, a minority owner of a house in Baltimore, said:

We have equal votes on day-to-day matters like who will do the cooking or cleaning. But on decisions like repairs or improvements which will affect the value of

*our asset, we vote according to our financial stake in
the house. It works out fine.*

**If one of you dies, how will the remaining owners keep up with
the mortgage payments?**

One solution, of course, would be to recruit another co-owner.
But you may not want to be forced into bringing in another partner
simply for fear of the debt collector. A better idea may be to buy inexpensive life insurance policies naming your co-owners as
beneficiaries. This is common among married couples when both
husband and wife are wage earners and neither income alone could
support a mortgage. It can easily be adapted to your group.

**How much time and money do you want to spend maintaining
or improving your house?**

If you are all accomplished tinkerers and the house you want
to buy is a true "handyman's special," then you've probably already
given a lot of thought to this question. Failure to discuss this issue
can create resentment later if one owner begins to press for improvements that are beyond the financial means of the others. One
solution could be to agree in advance on an annual repair and improvement budget. The agreement could even include a provision
for "sweat equity," allowing an owner to contribute labor to a project at hand at an agreed upon hourly rate.

**Who will own the major appliances and other furnishings in
the house?**

This should be spelled out in your agreement, even if ownership of them is to remain separate. This way a lot of bitterness can
be avoided in case of a falling out. You may want to treat your
stove, refrigerator, washer, and dryer as part of the property and
make them subject to the same terms of ownership. Where it is not
obvious who owns what, the ownership of other major items (e.g.,
televisions and stereos) can be spelled out in a series of addenda to
your principal agreement.

What happens if you all stop liking each other, but no one wants to move out of the house?

A simple provision is to agree to draw straws for the right to stay and buy out the shares of the other owners at a fair market value. Often the person staying will be allowed to make the buy-out payments over a period of several years.

What will you do if one person is unable or fails to make his monthly mortgage payment?

In this case, you could allow the other owners to make payment for the defaulting owner and increase their equity accordingly. If the reason for the default is simply a short-term problem of cash flow, you may want to permit the defaulting owner to make up the missed payment in a certain number of days and pay a small penalty to the other owners for the inconvenience.

How and where will records be kept of all transactions?

You may want to appoint one owner a record keeper, agreeing further that a monthly or quarterly accounting of all transactions will be made to each owner.

If it becomes necessary, how will you determine the value of your house?

Simple consensus is a good place to start, but it's important to have a back-up method of valuation if you aren't able to agree. One common method is to allow each other to select an independent real estate appraiser who will value the property. If the appraisers can't agree, then they in turn select a third appraiser who makes the final, binding valuation.

If you and your potential co-owners discuss and reach agreement on all of these questions, you have a good basis for a co-ownership contract. As you discuss the questions and turn them inside out, you'll probably think of additional ones. Take notes as you reach an agreement, then compose a draft agreement. At that point, because of the differences in property laws from state to state, it will be necessary to consult a lawyer. But you will have done all the ground work, and you'll be able to save the lawyer's time and your money. With your draft agreement in hand, it will be relatively easy for the lawyer to touch it up with a "to wit" here and an "undersigned" there.

Live-In Landlords

If you don't feel up to the headaches of shared ownership, but still want to own and live in a group house, there is an increasingly popular alternative: to buy a house yourself and then bring in housemates to share the place with you. Sometimes this situation is forced upon a person. A widowed or divorced person, for example, might suddenly have a lot of extra space and more limited financial circumstances. The immediate advantages of the owner-housemate arrangement are obvious. You'll be earning several hundred dollars a month in extra income, which will help offset the burden of monthly mortgage payments. In effect, your tenant-housemates will be buying your house for you. But the arrangement has its drawbacks, too. Wearing two hats, a landlord hat and a housemate hat, is no easy task. Marty, who is thirty-five and has owned a house and shared it with housemates for four years, posed a question:

Have you ever had a romance with your boss or someone who works for you? It's hard sorting out your professional from your personal attitudes. Being a landlord to your housemates is similar because if tension results from your landlord-tenant relationship it can disrupt the democratic atmosphere that group houses need.

From the point of view of the tenant-housemate, living with the landlord also has its pros and cons. The biggest advantage is that, with your landlord in the next bedroom, using the same kitchen and the same bathroom, you won't have a landlord with an "out-of-sight-out-of-mind" attitude. Have you ever rented a house or apartment and awakened to icy radiators in January, only to learn that your landlord is in Florida? Well, if you live with your landlord, when you freeze, he freezes.

There are other benefits. Dan, a renter in Houston, Texas, lived with a group of people who together owned their house. In the group situation, where his landlords became his friends, the resentment Dan had felt for previous landlords disappeared. "When you live in your friends' house," he said, "if something's wrong with the house, you can take out your tools and fix things. I don't like to do that at somebody else's house. I won't mind fixing up my room and helping them fix the house." Dan, with no financial stake of his own in the house, still caught the enthusiasm of his owner-housemates. The disadvantage for a tenant-housemate is simply the flip side of the "two-hat" problem. You may end up with a landlord who is so possessive that he becomes imperious. He'll ask you to turn down the stereo for the simple reason that it's his house.

It is possible to have a thoroughly satisfying housemate relationship between landlord and tenant. Like any other group house, success will flow from the ability of the group to anticipate and plan for problems and to clarify and state the relationship explicitly.

It is in the clarification area that landlords and tenants who live together need to do some extra work. Here are some of the questions that need to be considered:

Which decisions will the house make as a group? Which will the landlord reserve the right to make alone?

Probably the best arrangement is to let consensus rule day-to-day life. Obviously, no one would live with a landlord-housemate who insisted on telling people what and when they'd eat and who would do the cooking. Equally obvious is that the landlord-housemate will tend to set the tone of the house, simply because he'll be the first housemate and he'll select other housemates with expectations about the house that match his. In this way, the landlord stamps the character of the house, but after he chooses that second housemate he shouldn't choose number three without consulting number two.

There are decisions that must be the property owner's alone. Decisions on maintenance and improvements should be left to the landlord. The reason for this should be made clear to the tenants—the landlord has made a sizable down payment and has a big financial stake in his property. He will make all decisions that might affect its value.

How will the landlord justify the rent he charges. How will he explain a rent increase if it becomes necessary?

Of course, one answer to this question is that it's none of the tenant's business and that, in a free marketplace, the tenants should find another landlord if they don't like the one they have. But such a libertarian approach conflicts with the spirit of cooperation and interdependence that group living demands.

Marty says that he is open about his financial affairs with his housemates:

> *They're not idiots. I've had housemates who put their extra cash into the money market earning twelve per-cent interest. So they know that I deserve a return on my investment, too. If they thought I was gouging them, that would be different. But I'm not.*

Once the mechanical aspects of living with tenants or land-lords are dealt with, as they should be in advance, there remains the ongoing problem of overcoming the natural hesitation a tenant will feel about sharing space equally with the owner of that space.

One thing Alex kept in mind the whole time he lived with his landlord is useful to remember:

> *Whenever I felt a stir that I was treading on someone else's territory, I reminded myself that I paid good money every month to use that space and that it gave me certain rights, too. I also make a point of bringing some of my furniture and things into the common areas. That put other people in the positions of using my things.*

Having tenants as housemates has proved to be a real boon for some landlords. Terry has a large house in San Francisco and has several tenants living with him. As one of his housemates said, "The biggest plus to Terry about renting his house out is that if he didn't, he couldn't afford to stay home and write plays." Terry added a further twist—he reserved several bedrooms in the house and opened up a "bed and breakfast" service, primarily for young international travelers. His other housemates liked the novelty of the situation and appreciated the cultural aspect.

Can Housemates Hold Insurance Policies?

Group living has gone middle-class—Prosperous and upwardly mobile young people are living in group houses. They have stereos, color televisions, food processors, and valuable antiques that need to be insured. Yet insurance companies are still a little wary of writing insurance policies for groups; however, just about anything can be insured—for a price.

As a group, there are essentially two sorts of insurance that you might need. The first—life insurance as a means of mortgage protection—is touched on in an earlier section of this chapter. It has now become commonplace for a married couple, neither of whom could afford property separately, to purchase that property together and protect their investment with insurance policies naming each other as beneficiaries. It is becoming easier for groups to devise an expanded version of this arrangement.

A more problematical group insurance need is for renter's insurance. Here, it seems, insurance companies haven't gotten beyond the vision of group houses as freewheeling, Haight-Ashbury, "crash" pads. An agent for a large, national insurance company said that the high "traffic" through a group house was an open invitation to theft and accident. Apparently he did not think that a family with several teenagers probably presents a greater risk.

The image of group houses as high insurance risks has not died, but the need for groups to have fire, liability, and theft insurance in America's crime-ridden cities is increasing. The good news is that you can get insurance, though you must expect, depending on where you live, to pay a little more than the average nuclear family will. Each house member will probably have to buy a separate policy before any one of you will be allowed to hold insurance. "This," an agent said, "is to protect the insurance company against spurious claims filed by group house dwelling policyholders on behalf of their uninsured housemates."

If you move in with your landlord, the situation can be overcome beause the homeowner's insurance will cover the belongings of the rent-paying housemates.

The maxim that applies to all buying, and doubly to insurance, is "shop around." Rates will, of course, vary from state to state and from company to company.

Advanced Group Living: Scene 4, Better Living Through Barter

We expected something more than the usual group house, and when we turned the corner onto that street, our expectations were confirmed. Before us stood an imposing building that once contained fifteen apartments. It now houses a cooperative group fluctuating in membership between twenty-five and thirty.

We arrived for dinner at about 7:00. Marnie, our hostess, met us at the door and showed us around the ground floor where a wide central hall had at one time yielded to five "railroad" apartments. Renovation was taking place amid heaps of construction material.

Marnie led us into the front room on the left, which served as the house library. Several of the long-term house residents had pooled their books and, neatly arranged by topic, their combined collections filled shelves from ceiling to floor. A large bay window with a window seat faced the street.

Behind the library, away from the street, were rooms containing the offices of the computer company started by several house members. "We do software and data processing for several businesses and non-profit groups," Marnie explained. "They pay us or we barter. We get a lot of our construction material from a hardware store we do accounting for."

Barter comes into play in other areas of the house, too. Several members of the house bring skills to the group that they contribute to the renovation of the building. In turn, the group takes this work in lieu of rent.

Dinner was ready, so we joined other house members who were at home that evening in the large dining room. Seventeen people were already seated around a large table. Cooking chores are rotated among house members, and it takes a team of two to cook for this group. The kitchen looked more than adequate for the task. Two refrigerators and a six-burner gas stove suitable for a restaurant ringed the room. In a small dark chamber off the kitchen, a pantry overflowed with canned goods, grains, dried beans, potatoes, and onions.

The house members were a varied lot, ranging in age from men and women in their early twenties to an elderly woman in her sixties, who had lived in the building for years and decided to stay on after the building ceased to be an apartment building. Many of the housemates worked in public interest jobs, which appropriately complemented their communal living arrangement.

"The togetherness is terrific," said Rex, a carpenter who works full-time fixing up the house. "Sometimes I feel like we're all pioneers."

After dinner we talked more to Marnie about the computer operation, the aspect of the house that we found the most interesting. "I wouldn't say we're trying to leave the money economy altogether," Marnie said. "We're just trying to limit our involvement with it. The computer has enabled us to do that. We do computers on a level that can help the small retailer, who as a group are still a little afraid of the new technology. In turn, they're pleasantly surprised that we don't want cash for our services. So far our relationships with our clients have been mutually beneficial. Personally, I find it very satisfying. And we couldn't have done it without a group of people who really wanted to integrate all aspects of their lives."

C H A P T E R
S E V E N

Group Housing for Seniors: A Mini-Handbook

Men and Women in their twenties and thirties are not the only people living in group houses. Increasingly, and for many of the same reasons, people in their fifties, sixties, and seventies opt to share living quarters. And often, because of the financial and physical problems many senior citizens face, a church or community group sponsors the house and helps it cope with the more strenuous aspects of daily living.

Older people who live together enjoy the benefits anyone who shares enjoys: companionship and the opportunity to cut living expenses. But older people, especially those who for some reason can no longer live alone, can gain further benefits from sharing a house. Group living can provide one alternative to the hospital-like atmosphere of the nursing home.

To suggest that all seniors who share living space would otherwise be candidates for the nursing home presents a false picture, as the following examples show.

John Gibbons, aged seventy, had never married and lived most of his life in different boarding houses in Portland, Oregon. The owner of his last residence died, and the house was closed. For several weeks, John slept on a friend's couch at night and during the day looked for a room or apartment he could afford. He had no success. Then he heard about a vacancy in a house rented by three other retired men, and with some apprehension, he gave them a call. They invited him over for dinner. The three men found John to be a little withdrawn but were amused when he politely criticized the meal and suggested that his forty years experience as a short-order cook might be just what the house needed. The next day, they offered him the room, and he moved in that afternoon. John's shyness soon disappeared. Now, his housemates say, John will "talk your ear off," especially if you enter the kitchen, where he is the undisputed master.

Kathryn Gabel was eighty-two and living alone in a motel room on a diet of 400 milligrams of Miltown a day. She had no family and refused to enter a nursing home. She was, as *Newsweek* reported, "trying hard to die."[7] Share-a-Home, a network of senior group houses in Orlando, Florida, entered Kathryn Gabel's life. Among people who cared for her, Kathryn stopped taking medication and resumed a regular diet. She lived four more years before dying of a stroke.

In Cambridge, Massachusetts, four women who used to live in nursing homes now share an apartment. Student volunteers helped solicit funding for the project and arrange support services for the four women. The women, apprehensive about living alone, found in their cooperative arrangement an ideal alternative to insitutional care.

Harry Bracken, eighty-eight, had an extra room in his house and was willing to offer it to someone who would cook his dinner for him each evening. Through Operation Match of Montgomery County, Maryland, Mr. Bracken found Michael Israel, a retired crane operator who was looking for inexpensive accommodation in the Washington area. After five months, as Mr. Israel told a reporter from *The Washington Post*, the match was, "not too bad at all. I'm a little stubborn and he's a little stubborn."[8]

These examples only hint at the variety of solutions senior citizens have found to the housing dilemma they face, and there's no question that the situation is a serious one. Susan Stockard of the Boston Shared Living Project described this dilemma in written testimony presented in 1981 to the Select Committee on Aging of the U.S. House of Representatives:

> *As the elderly reach a point where living in a supportive community could be most beneficial, they often find themselves the most isolated. Death of spouses and friends, physical separation from children, the break-up of neighborhoods through renewal and condominium conversion, the need to move into more affordable housing, retirement and the subsequent loss of one's peer group, cut older people off from the community just when reliance on others is increased by more frequent long-term illness, reduction of physical stamina, and living on low or fixed incomes.*

Shared living has arisen as a partial solution to this problem. Americans prize independence, but as they age, frailty limits their ability to live independently. Care institutions threaten this independence. Group living provides a compromise based on the ideal of *interdependence*.

How Senior Group Living Differs

It is possible to find senior group arrangements that are indistinguishable from those younger people establish. But often senior groups are drawn together under the sponsorship of a community group. An important reason for sponsorship is economic need. When those who enter a group house are on fixed or low incomes, sponsorship is often required to defray some of the costs of the venture. The sponsor might be a church, synagogue, or government agency. Evidence that group living projects are an efficient use of taxpayers' money has persuaded governments at every level to get involved. In other cases, government organizations become involved when a use was demonstrated for unutilized resources. Christian Communities Group Homes, which provides support services to three group houses in Washington, D.C., wouldn't have been able to establish their program if the city hadn't donated three houses rent free.

Sponsorship is also necessary when the physical needs of the elderly have set up barriers to independence. Although group houses are not meant to be nursing homes, they must take these limitations into consideration while fostering independence through interdependence. The range of services that must be supplied of course depends on the requirements of the residents. As enumerated by Dennis Day-Lower of Philadelphia's Shared Housing Resource Center, Services may include homemaker/chore services, Meals-On-Wheels programs, community lunch programs, transportation services, visiting nurses or nurses aides, and management or house facilitation support.

How did group living for senior citizens come about? Who had the first senior group house? Although this question is impossible to answer, it's easy to imagine how an elderly group house might occur naturally.

Suppose Mr. and Mrs. Smith own a large house in the city,

small enough to have seemed crowded when they were raising their four children but cavernous once the children left home. Mr. Smith has an ample, but fixed, pension and in the face of rising property taxes and prices, it goes less and less far each year. Mrs. Smith's cousin, Mrs. Jones, lives alone in an apartment but is going deaf and has become fearful that she won't hear a fire alarm or will be robbed on a street in her neighborhood. She moves into one of the spare bedrooms in the Smith house, starts to sleep better at night, and as a bonus, pays only half the rent she paid before.

A few weeks later, a friend of Mrs. Jones from her old apartment building, whose husband has recently died, joins the Smiths and Mrs. Jones. Seeing the advantages of the new arrangement beginning to accrue, Mr. Smith puts a classified ad in the newspaper and finds a widower to complete the household. Not only have Mr. and Mrs. Smith made up the financial ground lost to inflation, but they have enough extra income to refurbish the basement, turning it into a comfortable accessory apartment. They rent their "English Basement" to a highly paid young professional just out of law school.

This one hypothetical example does not begin to express the variety of living arrangements that the elderly and agencies that sponsor senior shared living have devised. Four basic arrangements for senior group housing bear examination in more detail: "one-to-one" or "service exchange" house sharing, shared living, cooperative housing, and "intergenerational" group living.

One-to-One or Service Exchange Housesharing

From Washington, D.C., to Seattle, Washington, the one-to-one shared living arrangement is increasingly popular. While perhaps not technically within the definition of the group house expressed elsewhere in this book, the one-to-one solution is important for seniors because it is so common. According to the Stevens Housing Improvement Program in Seattle, Washington, 80 percent of the senior group houses they have helped establish fall into this category. The popularity of the arrangement can be attributed to two factors: many dwellings simply can't accomodate more than two people comfortably, and many people prefer the intimacy of the one-to-one match to the more complex interactions of a larger group.

Operation Match, administered by local government housing authorities throughout the greater Washington, D.C. area, is a good example of a program that has dedicated itself to bringing people together in one-to-one arrangements. They've had great success also with service exchange arrangements, like the one between Harry Bracken and Michael Israel.

Their typical match is like the one arranged for a woman, fifty-eight, who was forced to retire because of ill health soon after she bought a two-bedroom condominium. With expenses higher than her disability check, she went to Operation Match. They matched her with a widow who was returning to Washington but who couldn't find an apartment she could afford in her old neighborhood.

Shared Living Houses

In a shared living arrangement, typically three or more people will live together in a house that once housed a single family. Each person has a private bedroom, and common areas (including bathrooms, kitchen, and living rooms) are shared. Such an arrangement can occur naturally or can be organized by an institution or sponsoring agency. Since this is also the type of arrangement described throughout our book, you can refer to chapter 2 for advice on finding a house and housemates.

If the house is sponsored by a church, civic agency, or local government, the costs incurred to keep the house operating are often subsidized. Such costs include the salaries of cooks or housecleaners who come into the house to complete tasks beyond the physical stamina of the residents.

Cooperative Houses

This new approach to shared living for the elderly exists largely in the planning stage. One organization, Homesharing for Seniors, in Seattle, Washington, describes it as follows:

There is a new option we hope to offer soon. Not only can you share an entire house with two, three, four or more people, but you can own a part of the house, too. Our plans call for a housing cooperative made up of ten to fifteen houses which the residents will own as a group. This "co-op" option will enable the homesharers to make the decisions. The people who live in the houses can decide how to run the house, what color to paint it, and how to keep it up properly. The house will really be yours because you will be a co-owner.

The form which Homesharing hopes this ownership will take is similar to that of a cooperative apartment building. The houses will be owned by a non-profit corporation, and the residents will each own a share in the corporation. Presumably, if a shareholder wanted to sell his share and move out, he couldn't do so indiscriminately. A new shareholder would be carefully interviewed and selected by the other owners before the transaction could take place.

Intergenerational Group Housing

Intergenerational group living, while a less common arrangement is in many ways the most interesting. It has strong adherents such as Maggie Kuhn, the head of the Gray Panthers, who practices and preaches intergenerational group living. Writing several years ago about her house in *50 plus*, she said:

> *I love the vitality of these young people; having them around me re-energizes me, makes me feel more alive. What I have to offer them, hopefully, is a sense of experience and survivorship, which can help give perspective to their lives. These different qualities are the perennial qualities of the young and old, and when exchanged in friendship they give richness to all concerned.* [9]

Others take a more radical view, arguing that intergenerational group living could be the germ of a new revolution in social values.

Dean, a former engineer in his mid-fifties who recently came east from California to New York, presents this view forcefully. His views are very much an outgrowth of his life experience. Several years ago, Dean suffered a series of personal setbacks that showed him how fragile personal networks are and forced him to rethink many of his views of society. After the energy crisis of the early 1970s, Dean lost his job in an engineering firm closely linked to the oil industry. Soon after that his marriage began to break up. Dean realized then how alone he was, that he had been cut adrift from his friends at work and from friends he and his wife knew only as a couple.

Observing his own experience, Dean became interested in returning to school to study sociology. The subject that fascinated him most was the experience of aging in the United States, and especially the attitudes younger people have toward aging. He was struck by the fact that few people realize that the vast majority of seniors in this country are ambulatory, employed, fully functioning citizens, not bedridden, intrevenously-fed people waiting in nursing homes to die. At the same time, older people seem willing to accept the stigma our society places on aging.

Dean, who shares a house with a woman in her fifties and a woman in her twenties, now believes that our society needs to rethink its attitudes toward older people and to begin to recognize and encourage contribution from older people. Intergenerational housing is both a means and an end in this process.

First, Dean says, we need to eliminate the negative stigma associated with sharing one's house. The American Dream demands that we isolate ourselves in single-family homes, even after our children move away or our spouse dies. To allow others to enter out house as resident is a sign of failure. It's a confession to the world that we've turned our house, which is supposed to be a preserve from the world, into a business.

There are more reasons than simple economic ones to live intergenerationally. Dean sees such households as the ideal location for the development of mentor relationships. Through such relationships, survival techniques can be passed on from generation to generation. The young can express the problems they are encountering as they make an effort to get on in life, and the elderly can show the young that getting through difficult situations is not impossible and that many have encountered the same problems before.

As the older members of a household pass down their experience, the younger members can help the elder to live longer. By constantly bringing fresh ideas into the home, the young can keep the elderly from developing closed minds. And by donating their physical stamina to household tasks, the young can help to keep the household operating cheaply.

Through intergenerational housing, Dean sees the development of what he calls "the neo-nuclear family," a group combining the best of the fresh ideas of youth with the experience of the elderly, a group in which each member of the family is constantly rethinking his social attitudes so that each generation's stereotypes will be eliminated forever.

Starting a Senior Group House

If this chapter has sparked your interest in joining or helping to organize a senior group living project, the time has come to start planning. There are a lot of details to be worked out, and there will be a lot of expenses, so it's a good idea to involve as many people as possible. By now you've identified a need. You yourself may want to give group living a try, or you know someone who wants to, or you've noticed that many senior citizens in your community tolerate unsatisfactory living conditions.

Your next task is to show others that the need exists. A church, neighborhood association, club, or local council on aging can provide a ready forum for raising the issue. An announcement on a bulletin board or a short statement at a meeting could start the ball rolling. If nothing else comes of it, taking this first step may bring together people who want to share but don't really need any outside help. If others come forward and say that they'd like to try group living but are hesitant or that they've noticed the need, then you have the start of something. Only two or three more people are necessary to have a meeting, though perhaps at this preliminary stage it's best not to give your gathering that label. A meeting implies an agenda and decisions, but at this point, you are more interested in discussing the issue and exchanging views and ideas. Call it a *discussion group*. If you must decide anything, it's probably a simple decision about how best to go about enlarging your discussion group. The Association for Boston Community Development has good advice on how to achieve this preliminary goal:

*Organizers can seek the support and participation of
potential residents, other interested older (or younger)
people, neighborhood residents, local government of-
ficials, etc. Community action agencies, councils on aging, agencies for the aged, housing authorities, home-
care agencies, local senior clubs, congregate dining
clubs, churches and synagogues are all places to look
for support and participation.*

When you plan with a large group of people, you'll find strong disagreements. Full agreement is rare, but you will accomplish more with help from others than you will if planning is a jealously guarded preserve of a select minority. If consensus can be reached, everyone will believe their ideas are respected, and everyone will pull together on the project. Time given willingly and cheerfully will be one of your most valuable assets. For more on consensus decision-making, see Chapter 3.

Sooner or later, if your discussion group is to go beyond the debating society level, you'll have to get down to the nitty gritty. The four issues on which you will have to make hard decisions are site, funding, support, and recruitment.

Choosing a Site

The location of the house or apartment you choose is an ex-tremely important consideration; so is its physical layout. They are important factors because of the physical needs and limitations many senior citizens have. Psychological factors also come into play. Further, site is closely tied to our pocket books. All of us would like to live in Buckingham Palace, but few of us could afford it.

When evaluating the location of a prospective dwelling, you should ask youself the following questions: Is the house or apart-ment close to parks and stores? Is public transportation convenient-ly nearby? What sort of neighborhood is it? Will the house residents feel safe there?

Inside the house, you should ask more questions: Are the electrical and plumbing systems in good condition? If not, what sort of repairs will be necessary? How much will they cost? If any of the prospective residents are not as strong or mobile as they once were, will the layout of the house hinder them? How many ramps, smoke alarms, bathroom grab bars, or other alterations do you need? How much will they cost?

Lastly, evaluate the site as a place where interacting humans will reside: How many people will move in the house? Where can they gather? Where can they sit alone if they prefer? The layout of the site should facilitate the residents' desires to interact or to remain somewhat independent, depending on what they prefer to do.

These are a lot of questions to ask, and,as you can see, some of them are quite complex. Site identification and selection is a time when professional help can be very useful. Help can come very cheaply. If you can, entice an architect to join your study group. Is there a graduate school of architecture in your town or city? If so, consider approaching its faculty. Perhaps they'll give their students credit for doing your work for you.

Finding Funding

The questions you must ask when evaluating a site may be answered in part by your financial resources. With the economies that sharing brings, even seniors in an unsponsored group can usually afford the costs of their living situation. But imagine a sponsored house for low-income senior citizens, some of whom have physical disabilities. At one end of the scale, a house of this type requires some sort of rental subsidy, to cover the expensive alterations in the physical structure of the building. So what you can and can't do in your senior group living project depends a great deal on how much money you have. However, the sources of money are almost as varied as opinions of how to spend it, as the following examples indicate.

In Cambridge, Massachusetts, students from Harvard's social

service organization, Philips Brooks House, organized the Elder Cooperative Housing Option (ECHO). They obtained a rent subsidy from the Cambridge Housing Authority and, eventually, a CETA block grant for their project.

In Boston, the Volunteers of America combined interest on their own assets with house residents' Supplemental Security Income (SSI) to fund a senior group house.

In Florida, at the granddaddy of all organized senior shared living projects, Florida Share-a-Home, residents make monthly contributions according to their financial ability. As *Life* magazine described it in 1972:

> *The members' contributions range from $200 to $375 a month, compared to $800 and up each month for a room in a decent nursing home. The contribution covers a monthly payment of $800 to the previous owner of the house,... heat, utilities, food, laundry, field trips [and] transportation.* [10]

Money is available from federal, state, and local governments, but these sources are growing more scarce. Check with your state housing authority or your local Housing and Urban Development (HUD) office for information about Section 8 rent subsidies. A Boston woman who started a group house after she was forced to close her boarding house was able to obtain Section 8 assistance despite the fact that the regulations limited assistance to families.

Money is nice, but only useful for what it buys you. The point is, it is also possible to skip the middleman and go right to the source. If you are renovating a house, for example, donations of material and volunteer time are worth a lot of dollars.

Seeking Support

"Support" means the outside help your group house will need to operate on a day-by-day or week-by-week basis. It could be

Elderly Group Living Questionnaire Guide

1. Basic Information: Name, Age, Address, Length of Residence
2. Next of kin, Contact in case of Emergency
3. Employment, Salary, Other Income, Large or Unusual Expenses
4. Living Experience: Have you ever lived with people not related to you for a significant piece of time? Have you had to share important facilities such as bathrooms?
5. Hobbies, Favorite Chore, Least Favorite Chore
6. Physical Disabilities: Does climbing stairs present a difficulty? Can you bathe yourself? How far can you walk without resting?
7. Personal Likes (Dislikes): Bedtime, Noise
8. Medication, Medical History, Diet
9. Attitudes toward Sharing, Need for Privacy

nothing more than having a volunteer come once a week in the summer to mow the lawn. But it could be extremely elaborate—homemakers who clean and cook hot meals, drivers who take residents shopping or to the library or recreation center, and repairmen who fix things. Support can also include a social worker who comes weekly to facilitate a group meeting at which problems are aired and decisions are made.

Analyze the needs of your group. Finances, as usual, are a constraint, but they don't have to choke you. If the other service needs of your house can be met by volunteers, perhaps you can afford a part-time homemaker.

Recruiting Members

Recruitment is a delicate and complicated process. If you're organizing a senior group living project without specific individuals in mind, then you'll have to find and match compatible people. You can spread the word with leaflets and advertisements at nursing homes and social service agencies. One group studied the demography of its neighborhood and located potential residents by comparing police listings with lists of boarding house residents. Once someone expresses interest, a lot of time can be saved by having him or her complete an application form. The questions and topics listed in the questionnaire guide should help you to write the form your organization needs.

After screening applicants, bring the most suitable ones together to meet one another. This interaction gives them a chance to test their own compatibility and to see whether they want to continue the application process.

Once you've made your final selection, and as you add people later to fill vacancies, you may want to make the first thirty days of residency a trial period.

House Dynamics

In a sponsored group house, you've only just begun when your residents move in. Aside from the more mundane chores of house operations, helping the housemates get along can be a time-consuming job.

A good way to start is by having the residents work out house rules for themselves. Catholic Social Services of Honolulu said:

> We help the ... matched people to work out a written agreement before beginning to live together. This agreement covers expectations on sharing the kitchen, cooking, housework, any work in the house (in exchange for rent), etc. We feel writing these expectations down is conducive to a smooth match.

The extent to which the sponsoring agency becomes involved in relations among house members depends on the philosophy of the sponsor and the independence of the residents. A "managed" approach is arguably in contradiction to the whole aim of group living. Rather than fostering independence, it may lead to a feeling among residents of loss of control.

A "participatory" approach, on the other hand, permits residents to be masters of their own house, yet outside help doesn't disappear altogether. A common kind of help is for a trained facilitator to come into the house for a weekly house meeting. Many people will be living in a democratic situation for the first time, and so learning to settle for less than what they most want is a difficult adjustment. A facilitator helps the residents communicate and focus on the true source of conflicts.

But a house meeting is more than just a gripe session, it's also where plans are made. Decisions about new residents, organizing a birthday party, planning a group trip out of town—all of these and more can be a part of the agenda of a group meeting.

Why We Like it Here—Some Testimonies from Senior Housemates

The evidence strongly supports the viability and desirability of group living for seniors. From Homesharing for Seniors, Seattle, Washington:

> *You can't measure all the homesharing benefits in dollars and cents. . . . It's worth an awful lot to get a good night's sleep because there's another person in the house.*

From Share-A-Home in Orlando, Florida, as described in *Life* Magazine:

> *When (Joe) McInerny feels like talking about the old days now, or about his son and grandchildren, he can usually find someone who is eager to listen and learn. That's a lot different, he says, from the way it was in the nursing home. Living here, McInerny is also able to come and go as he pleases. Usually he eats at one of the two large tables in the dining room; sometimes he goes out with friends to seafood restaurants.* [11]

From Catholic Social Service of Honolulu:

> *Our programs have been successful. Small Group Homes (SGH) is expanding up to eight to ten homes next year. Handicapped seniors have shown some remarkable improvements after joining SGH. One*

woman was uncertain whether she could cook and had great difficulty walking (with a walker). After one month in an SGH, she is cooking, beginning to walk outside the house, and has set herself the goal of walking a half mile to a nearby shopping center. She says that for the first time in two years, she feels she has something to look forward to and to live for. Having friends around her and program support has improved her physical capability dramatically. By forming a family-like support group, the seniors have found they could remain independent longer than if they had been living alone.

Appendix I
A Directory of Roommate Referral Services Across the United States

ARIZONA

Roommate Finders
4747 N. 16th St. Suite A 117
Phoenix, AZ 85016
(602) 264-0809

Room Finders
2043 N. 16th St.
Phoenix, AZ 85006
(602) 258-0463

Bette's Old Time
Matchmaking
P.O. Box 8560
Phoenix, AZ 85040
(602) 237-2658

Roommate Finders of Tucson
630 N. Craycroft Rd.
Tucson, AZ 85711
(602) 790-7666

CALIFORNIA

D.U.S.E. (Double Up Share
   Expenses)
8146 Greenback Lane,
Suite 204
Fair Oaks, CA 95628
(916) 969-3873

Rent Sharers
937 Howe Ave.
Sacramento, CA 95825
(916) 924-0783

Original San Francisco
   Roommate Referall
610 Cole St.
San Francisco, CA 94117
(415) 626-0606

Community Rentals
470 Castro
San Francisco, CA 94114
(415) 552-8868

Rent-A-Rental
43 Franklin St.
San Francisco, CA 94102
(415) 863-9840

SHARE The Perfect Place
785 Market
San Francisco, Ca 94102
(415) 957-0772

Marin Roommates Bureau
219 East Blithedale Ave.
Marin Valley, CA
(415) 383-1161

Roommates Unlimited
1457 Woodside Rd.
Redwood City, CA 94061
(415) 365-3082

The Berkeley Connection
2840 College Ave.
Berkeley, CA 94705
(415) 845-7821

You Ask For It
27 N. San Mateo Drive
San Mateo, CA 94401
(415) 344-1705

Housemates Unlimited
6513 Hollywood Boulevard,
   Room 203
Los Angeles, CA 90028
(213) 466-8143

Room-Away Student
  Housing Exchange
8830 Rayford Drive
Los Angeles, CA 90045
(213) 649-3959

Roommate Finders, Inc.
100 Driftwood, Suite 15
Marina Del Ray, CA 90291
(213) 822-5548

Roommate Finders, Inc.
2901 Wilshire Blvd.
Santa Monica, CA 90291
(213) 453-1861

Roommate Finders Inc.
4348 Van Nuys Blvd.,
Suite 206
Sherman Oaks, CA 91403
(213) 990-5037

Roommate Finders, Inc.
330 North Central
Glendale, CA 91203
(213) 500-1656

Roommate Matchers
1930 11th St.
Santa Monica, CA 90404
(213) 452-2019

Roommate Finders
3713 Highland Ave.
Manhattan Beach, CA 90266
(213) 546-2563

The Rental Bank
4842 Van Nuys Blvd.
Sherman Oaks, CA 91423
(213) 783-7368

Housemates Unlimited
17341 Irvine, Suite 112
Tustin, CA 92680
(714) 832-4134

Roommate Finders, Inc.
5845 Westminster Blvd.
Westminster, CA 92683
(714) 895-3482

Roommate Finders, Inc.
4341 Birch
Newport Beach, CA 92660
(714) 641-1899

COLORADO

Find-A-Roommate
5650 E. Evans Ave.
Suite 209
Denver, CO 80222
(303) 692-9580

CONNECTICUT

Options: The Roommate
  Service
1707 Summer
Stamford, CT 06905
(203) 348-0919

Roommates Inc.
59 Amity Rd.
New Haven, CT 06525
(203) 389-0031

The Roommate Exchange
25 Jesup Rd.
Westport, CT 06881
(203) 222-0872

ARC Roommate Consultants
2377 Main
Glastonbury, CT 06033
(203) 633-0396

HomeShare
604 Federal Rd.
Brookfield, Ct 06804
(203) 775-6377

DISTRICT OF COLUMBIA

Roommates Preferred
702 Independence Ave., S.E.
Washington, D.C. 20003
(202) 547-4666

The Women's Information
Bank
3918 W. St., N.W.
Washington, D.C. 20007
(202) 333-9696

FLORIDA

Roommate Finders, Inc.
601 W. Oakland Park Blvd.
Ft. Lauderdale, FL 33311
(305) 563-6667

Roommate Referalls of Miami
8600 Northwest 53rd Terrace
Suite 213
Miami, FL 33175
(305) 559-1555

A Roommate Service
1776 E. Sunrise Ave.
Miami, FL 33133
(305) 525-1802

Roommate Finders
3252 S. Dixie Highway
Miami, FL 33133
(305) 448-5299

Match Makers, Inc.
10125 S.W. 72nd St.
Miami, FL 33173
(305) 524-6777

Apartment Paymates
2145 N.W. 5th Ave.
Gainesville, FL 32603
(904) 377-7799

Two Peas in a Pod
1472 Gulf to Bay Blvd.
Clearwater, FL 33515
(813) 461-7208

GEORGIA

Atlanta Student Housing Corp.
2159 Coosewate Dr.
Atlanta, GA 30319
(404) 634-7695

Apartment Finders/Roommate
  Finders
2531 Briarcliff Rd., N.E.
Atlanta, GA 30329
(404) 633-3331

Ray's Roommate Match Service
2285 Peachtree Rd., Suite 210
Atlanta, GA 30309
(404) 351-6991

HAWAII

Matching Roommates
1946 Young, Suite 480
Oahu, HI 96826
(808) 949-6421

Roommate Locators
1531 S. Beretania, Suite 204
Oahu, HI 96826
(808) 955-4428

LOUISIANA

Roommate Referalls, Inc.
1236 Decatur
New Orleans, LA 70116
(504) 525-4640

Roommates Found
3925 N I-10 Service Rd. (West)
Metairie, LA 70002
(504) 456-6606

MARYLAND

Christian Oasis
1010 Rockville Pike
Rockville, MD 20852
(301) 468-0120

Roommate Referalls of
   Columbia
5478 Mystic Court
Columbia, MD 21044
(301) 730-7722

The Housing Connection
P.O. Box 10554
Towson, MD 21204
(301) 583-9482

MASSACHUSSETTS

Matching Room-Mates, Inc.
251 Harvard Ave.
Boston, MA 02146
(617) 734-6409

Shared Living Project
67 Newbury
Boston, MA 02116
(617) 266-3814

MICHIGAN

Roommate Referral Service
3612 Partridge St.
Ypsilanti, MI 48197
(313) 971-4606

Home-Mate Specialists
30555 Southfield Rd.
Southfield, MI 48076
(313) 644-6845

Share Referral Service
884 S. Adams Rd.
Birmingham, IM 48011
(313) 642-1620

Preferred Roommates
11643 S. Saginaw
Grand Blanc, MI 48439
(313) 695-1832

MINNESOTA

Roommate Locator Services
   of Minneapolis & St. Paul

7250 France Ave. S.
Minneapolis, MN 55435
(612) 830-0900

MISSOURI

Roommate Search, Inc.
1231 Cheverly
St. Louis, MO 63143
(314) 878-9922

Roommate Finders
4116-A Pennsylvania Ave.
Kansas City, MO 64111
(816) 756-1556

Rent Splitters
1920 Swift
Kansas City, MD 64116
(816) 474-7097

NEBRASKA

Roommate Finders, Inc.
7171 Mercy Rd.
Omaha, NE 68106
(402) 397-8150

NEW JERSEY

Two's Company
419 Essex
Hackensack, NJ 07601
(201) 488-0608

NEW MEXICO

Roommate Finders for
  Albuquerque

10832J Prospect, N.E.
Albuquerque, NM 87108
(505) 296-6446

NEW YORK

The Gay Roommate Service
156 W. 74th St.
New York, NY 10023
(212) 580-7696

Roommate Finders
315 5th Ave.
New York, NY 10016
(212) 686-9870

Leslie Harper Co.
445 E. 80th St.
New York, NY 10021
(212) 794-9494

New York Roommate Service
515 Madison Ave.
Suite 903 at 53rd St.
New York, NY 10022
(212) 759-4203

Women's Roommate Referrals,
  Inc.
527 Madison Ave.
New York, NY 10022
(212) 888-6360

OHIO

Share-A-Home
4427 Talmadge Rd.
Toledo, OH 43623
(419) 385-0180

Roommate Placement Service
179 E. Macmillan
Cincinnati, OH 45219
(513) 381-0020

OKLAHOMA

Roommate Finders
5201 S. Western
Oklahoma City, OK 73109
(405) 682-4681

OREGON

Housemates Register
2405 N.W. Irving
Portland, OR 97210
(503) 225-1077

SOUTH CAROLINA

Roommate Finders
1900 Broad River Rd.
Columbia, SC 29210
(803) 731-9737

TENNESSEE

Nashville Roommate Service
120 Lanewood Ct.
Nashville, TN 37211
(615) 834-6603

TEXAS

A-1 Roommate Service
2629 Fountain View

Houston, TX 77057
(713) 266-3289

A-1 Roommate Service
1411 Spillers
Houston, TX 77043
(713) 932-1363

Room Mates
5619 Council Grove Lane
Houston, TX 77088
(713) 447-7006

Apartment Roommate Finders
4814 West Avenue, Suite 110
San Antonio, TX 78213
(512) 344-1212

Roommate Connections
400 East Anderson Lane
Suite 208
Austin, TX 78752
(512) 452-0420

Roommate Network
2813 Rio Grande, Suite 206
Austin, TX 78705
(512) 473-2800

Roommates of America
12200 Park Central Drive
Suite 111
Dallas, TX 75251
(214) 458-7227

UTAH

Matching Roommates
700 East 515 South,
Suite 2-H
Salt Lake City, UT 84107
(801) 322-5290

VIRGINIA

Metro Roommate Service
4901 Seminary Rd., Suite 105
Alexandria, VA 22311
(703) 998-4000

Roommate Finders
416 Virginia Ave.
Harrisonburg, VA 22801
(703) 433-3044

Roommaters
200 E. Nine Mile Rd.
Richmond, VA 23223
(804) 737-0422

WASHINGTON

Roommate Referral
W2028 Northwest Blvd.
Spokane, WA 99205
(509) 328-9877

WISCONSIN

Apartment-Roommate Search
5005 Monona Drive
Madison, WI 53716
(608) 221-9444

Roommates Ltd.
5110 West Bluemount Rd.
Milwaukee, WI 53208
(414) 259-9500

Appendix II
A Directory of Organizations which set up Senior Shared Living Arrangements*

*Some of the listed organizations may not set up senior houses but function as information centers for seniors interested in shared living.

CALIFORNIA

Alternate Living for the Aged
10345 West Pico Blvd.
Los Angeles, CA 90064

California Jewish Home
7150 Tampa Ave.
Resada, CA 91355

Housemates Unlimited
1731 Irvine, Suite 112
Tustin, CA 92680

Jewish Family & Children's
  Services
1600 Scott St.
San Francisco, CA 94115

Jewish Homes for the Aged
  of Greater Los Angeles
18855 Victory Blvd.
Resada, CA 91335

McGarr Senior Center
46 Mariposa Ave.
San Anselmo, CA 94960

Project Match
277 W. Hedding St.
San Jose, CA 95110

COLORADO

Geriatric Residential Program
1600 W. 24th St.
Pueblo, CO 81003

1390 Housing Inc.
P.O. Box 10848
Edgemont Branch
Golden, CO 80401

DELAWARE

Brandywine House
1901 Market St.
Wilmington, DE 19801

St. Patrick's House
107 E. 14th St.
Wilmington, DE 19801

Delaware Division of Aging
2407 Lancaster Ave.
Dover, DE 19901

DISTRICT OF COLUMBIA

Christian Communities Group
  Homes
1419 V. St. N.W.
Washington, DC 20009

Richmond Fellowship
1829 Kalorama Rd.
Washington, DC 20009

(Publish report: *Shared Housing
  for Older People)*

FLORIDA

Share-a-Home
701 Driver Ave.
Winter Park, FL 32789

GEORGIA

Jewish Family & Children's
  Bureau
1753 Peachtree Rd., N.E.
Atlanta, GA 30309

HAWAII

Small Group Homes for Adults
250 S. Vineyard St.
Honolulu, HI 96813

ILLINOIS

Council for Jewish Elderly
1015 Howard St.
Evanston, IL 60202

KENTUCKY

Union Labor Housing
1235 S. 3rd Street
Louisville, KY 40203

MARYLAND

Group Home Program
611 Montrose Rd.
Rockville, MD 20852

Home Care Research Inc.
36 E. Patrick St.
Frederick, MD 21701
(Publish a handy guide: *The
Three-in-One House)*

Hurwitz House
133 Slade Ave.
Baltimore, MD 21208

Operation Match
Housing Opportunities
  Commission
1400 Fenwick La.
Silver Spring, MD 20910

Small Group Home Project
5750 Park Heights Ave.
Baltimore, MD

MASSACHUSETTS

Action for Boston Community
  Development
178 Tremont St.
Boston, MA 12110
(They publish a very useful and
comprehensive guide: *Planning
and Developing a Shared Living
Project: A Guide for Community Groups)*

Amherst Congregate Housing
70 Bottwood Walk
Amherst, MA 01002

Amherst Congregate Housing
33 Kellogg Ave.
Amherst, MA 01002

Belknap House
207 Main St.
Concord, MA 01742

Bradford Russell Home
62 Centre St.
Fairhaven, MA 02719

Congregate Housing of the
Barnstable Housing Authority
Pine & South Sts.
Hyannis, MA 02601

Cooperative Living of Newton
474 Centre St.
Newton, MA 02158

Elder Cooperative Living
Options/Cahill II
1493 Cambridge St.
Cambridge, MA 02139

Congregate Housing Facility
116 Norfolk St.
Cambridge, MA 02139

Project SHARE
233 Harvard St.
Brookline, MA 02146

Shared Living Project
67 Newbury St.
Boston, MA 02116

Somerville Housing Authority
30 Memorial Rd.
Somerville, MA 02142

MISSOURI

Jewish Federation of
Saint Louis
411 North Seventh St.
Suite 1700
Saint Louis, MO 63101

NEW JERSEY

Cooperative Living
Arrangements
164 Oak St.
Hohokus, NJ 07423

First Baptist Manor
Maple at Cove Rd.
Pennsauken, NJ 08109

Harel House
Pleasant Valley Home
115 Pleasant Valley Way
West Orange, NJ 07052

NEW YORK

Apartment Residence of
Westchester
Jewish Community Services
172 S. Broadway
White Plains, NY 10583

Apartment-Sharing Project
Lenox Hill Neighborhood
Association
331 E. 70th St.
New York, NY 10021

CSS Enriched Housing Program
2705 Schley Ave.
Bronx, NY 10465

Enriched Housing Project of
Schenectady
1248 Wendell Ave.
Schenectady, NY 12308

Mil-Benski Farm
6769 Miller Rd.
Newark, NY 14513

Project Share
129 Jackson St.
Hempstead, NY 11550

OHIO

Parker Morrow House
173 Front
Groveport, OH 43125

PENNSYLVANIA

Community Housing for the
  Elderly
Philadelphia Geriatric Center
5301 Old York Rd.
Philadelphia, PA 19141

Shared Housing Resource
  Center
6344 Greene St.
Philadelphia, PA 19144
(A national consulting service
promoting intergenerational
housing alternatives for older
people.)

RHODE ISLAND

Cooperative Living Project
126 Pierce St.
East Greenwich, RI 02818

WASHINGTON

Homesharing for Seniors
532 19th Ave.
Seattle, WA 98112
(Publish report: *Under One
Roof*)

WEST VIRGINIA

Good Living
4102 Fallam Dr.
Malden, WV 25306

WISCONSIN

Colonial House
124 Dewey St.
Sun Prairie, WI 53590

Appendix III
Books and
Resources for the
Shared Life

Cookbooks

Brown, Edward Espe. *The Tassajara Bread Book*. Boulder: Shambhala, 1970.

Claiborne, Craig. *The New New York Times Cookbook*. New York: Times Books, 1979.

Ewald, Ellen Buchman. *Recipes for a Small Planet*. New York: Ballantine, 1973.

Franey, Pierre. *The New York Times 60 Minute Gourmet*. New York: Fawcett Columbine, 1979.

Harrington, Geri. *The New College Cookbook*. New York: Grosset & Dunlap, 1982.

Katzen, Mollie. *The Moosewood Cookbook*. Berkeley: Ten Speed Press, 1971.

Rombauer, Irma S., and Becker, Marion R. *The Joy of Cooking*. Indianapolis: Bobbs-Merrill, 1975.

Thomas, Anna. *The Vegetarian Epicure*. New York: Knopf, 1980.

Thomas, Anna. *The Vegetarian Epicure Book Two*. New York: Knopf, 1980.

Energy Savers

Blandy, Thomas, and Lamoureux, Denis. *All Through the House: A Guide to Weatherization*. New York: McGraw-Hill, 1980.

Dubin, Fred S., and Robinson, Steven. *The Energy Efficient Home*. New York: New American Library, 1978.

Jones, Peter, *The Electrician's Bible*. Garden City, NY: Doubleday, 1982.

Scientific Staff of the Massachusetts Audubon Society. *The Energy Saver's Handbook for Town and City People*. Emmaus, PA: Rodale Press, 1982.

Time-Life Books Editors. *Fireplaces and Woodstoves*. Alexandria, VA: Time-Life, 1981.

In and Around the House

Cassidy, Bruce. *The Carpenter's Bible*. Garden City, NY: Doubleday, 1982.

Conran, Terence. *The House Book*. New York: Crown, 1982.

Crockett, James Underwood. *Crockett's Victory Garden*. Boston, Little, Brown & Co., 1977.

DiDonna, Lupe, and Sperling, Phyllis. *How to Design and Build Your Own House*. New York: Knopf, 1981.*

Druse, Kenneth. *Free Things for Gardeners.* New York: Perigee, 1982.

Grady, Tom, ed. *Free Stuff for Home and Garden.* Deephaven, MN: Meadowbrook Press, 1981.

Hennessey, James, and Papanek, Victor. *Nomadic Furniture 1.* New York: Pantheon, 1973.

Lane Publishing Company Editors. *How to Make Bookshelves and Cabinets.* Menlo Park, CA: Lane Publishing Co., 1980.

Moore, Alma Chestnut. *How to Clean Everything: an Encyclopedia of What to Use and How to Use It.* New York: Simon and Schuster, 1977.

Philbin, Tom. *Home Fix-It Secrets of the Pros.* New York: E.P. Dutton, 1980.

Pinkham, Mary Ellen. *Mary Ellen's Best of Helpful Kitchen Hints.* New York: Warner, 1980.

Pinkham, Mary Ellen. *Mary Ellen's Best of Helpful Hints Book Two.* New York: Warner, 1981.

Reader's Digest Editors. *Back-to-Basics.* Pleasantville, NY: Reader's Digest, 1981.

Reader's Digest Editors. *Do it Yourself Manual.* New York: Reader's Digest, 1973.

Reader's Digest Editors. *Fix It Yourself Manual.* New York: Reader's Digest, 1977.

Roda, Janet. *No Sew Decorating.* New York: Delta Dell, 1981.

Rooney, William F. *Practical Guide to Home Restoration.* New York: Bantam, 1981.

Schremp, William E. *Designer Furniture Anyone Can Make.* New York: Simon and Schuster, 1972.

Thomas, Diane. *Backyard Roughing It Easy.* New York: Fawcett Columbine, 1980.

Vellela, Tony. *Food Co-Ops for Small Groups.* New York: Workman, 1975.

Your Money and Your Rights

Blumburg, Richard E., and Grow, James R. *The Rights of Tenants.* New York: Avon, 1978.

Furcolo, Foster, L.L.B. *The New Practical Law for the Layman.* Washington, D.C.: Acropolis, 1982.

Hughes, Alan. *A Home of Your Own for the Least Cash.* Washington, D.C.: Acropolis, 1982.

Nickerson, Clarence B. *The Accounting Handbook for Non-Accountants.* Boston: CBI Publishing Co., 1979.

Books No Group House Should Be Without

Frishman, Dr. Austin M. *The Cockroach Combat Manual*. New York: Morrow, 1980.

Heatter, Maida. *Maida Heatter's Book of Great Desserts*. New York: Knopf, 1974.

The Mister Boston Deluxe Official Bartender's Guide. New York: Warner, 1979.

Trudeau, G.B. *The Doonesbury Chronicles*. New York: Holt, Rhinehart & Winston, 1975.**

Wallechinsky, David, and Wallace, Irving. *The People's Almanac*. New York: Bantam, 1981.**

* If you *really* want to start a house from scratch!
** Bathroom Literature

Footnotes

1. Maggie Kuhn, "Why Old and Young Should Live Together," *50 Plus* 18 (October 1978): 18-20.

2. Saul V. Levine, M.D., F.R.C.P. (C), Robert P. Carr, M.D., and Wendy Horenblas, B.S., "The Urban Commune: Fact or Fad, Promise or Pipedream?" *The American Journal of Orthopsychiatry* 43 (January 1973): 149-163.

3. Ibid.

4. Sharon Johnson, "Single Parents Try Out the Shared Life," *The New York Times,* 21 August 1979, p. C13.

5. D. Kelly Weisberg, "The Cinderella Children," *Psychology Today* 10 (April 1977): 84-6, 103.

6. George Williamson, "A Second Look at the Family," *San Francisco Chronicle,* 19 January 1978, p. 24.

7. M.A. Kellog and A. Jaffe, "Old Folks' Commune: Share-a-Home Network in Orlando, Florida," Newsweek 87 (19 April 1977): 97-8.

8. Sandra Evans Teeley, "Housing Two on a Match," *The Washington Post,* 7 November 1981, p. E1.

9. Maggie Kuhn, "Why Old and Young Should Live Together," *50 Plus* 18 (October 1978): 18-20.

10. M. James, "Commune for Old Folks; Share-a-Home Association of Winter Park, Florida," *Life* 72 (12 May 1972): 53-4.

11. Ibid.

INDEX